THE ARIZONA TRIVIA BOOK

By JAMES E. COOK

Gem Guides Book Company
315 Cloverleaf Dr., Suite F
Baldwin Park, California 91706

The Arizona Trivia Book
Copyright © 1991 by Gem Guides Book Company

Published in the United States of America.

ISBN 0-935182-51-9

PREFACE

There's more to Arizona than meets the eye of the casual visitor.

The state may seem at first to have only a short, explosive history. But Arizona's modern history goes back to Spanish explorers of 1539, and its beguiling prehistory is suggested in the ruins of civilizations much older than that.

Desert? Arizona has an ample supply. But the state's terrain is as varied as that of any western state, including several kinds of desert, vast pine forests and alpine peaks. Its canyons are some of the most spectacular on earth.

To this rich setting have come a marvelous assortment of heroes, outlaws, scientists, artists, entertainers, moviemakers, sportsmen, chasers of rainbows, and pilgrims seeking new life in the benign winter sunshine.

All contributed to *The Arizona Trivia Book.* For more than half a century, the author has prowled Arizona's rugged face and musty archives. He hopes you'll share his fascination with his native state.

Dedication

Q. What do Jerry, Julie, Jessica, Jennifer, Jacqueline and Joanne have in common?

A. I love them, and dedicate this book to them.

TABLE OF CONTENTS

GEOGRAPHY

C H A P T E R   O N E

Q. Which of Arizona's original four counties was known as the "mother of counties?"

A. Yavapai.

————?¿————

Q. Which is Arizona's newest county, formed in 1983?

A. La Paz.

————?¿————

Q. What historic county was split to form La Paz County?

A. Yuma County.

————?¿————

Q. What county contains more than half of Arizona's population?

A. Maricopa.

————?¿————

Q. What is Arizona's smallest county?

A. Santa Cruz.

————?¿————

Q. Which Arizona county is second largest in the nation?

A. Coconino.

Geography

Q. Where did Phoenix rank among American cities as of 1990?

A. Tenth largest.

———— ?¿ ————

Q. How does Arizona rank among U.S. states in land area?

A. Sixth largest.

———— ?¿ ————

Q. What natural disasters, calculated to happen once every century, devastated parts of Arizona in 1978, 1979, 1980 and 1983?

A. 100-year floods.

———— ?¿ ————

Q. What direction does the Colorado River flow as it leaves Yuma?

A. West-northwest.

———— ?¿ ————

Q. White River and Black River join to form what river?

A. Salt River.

———— ?¿ ————

Q. The Vermilion Cliffs parallel what river gorge across northern Arizona?

A. Marble Canyon on the Colorado River.

———— ?¿ ————

Q. What feature seven miles west of Flagstaff divides the waters of the Verde and Little Colorado River watersheds?

A. The Arizona Divide.

Geography

Q. What was the number of the U.S. Highway that called itself "The Main Street Of America?"

A. U.S. Route 66.

———?¿———

Q. U.S. Highway 60 crosses what spectacular canyon between Show Low and Globe?

A. Salt River Canyon.

———?¿———

Q. The Colorado River broke out of its banks south of Yuma in 1906, creating what California feature?

A. The Salton Sea.

———?¿———

Q. Most of the city of Yuma lies directly east of what state?

A. Baja California, Mexico.

———?¿———

Q. What river joins the Colorado at Yuma?

A. The Gila.

———?¿———

Q. How many national forests are there in Arizona?

A. Six.

———?¿———

Q. What Arizona forest is relatively devoid of foliage?

A. Petrified Forest.

———?¿———

Q. Arizona borders what state of Mexico?

A. Sonora.

Geography

Q. The rock formation called Cochise Head is in what range of mountains?

A. Chiricahuas.

——— ?¿ ———

Q. What is the newest name of the vast southwestern Arizona gunnery range established during World War II?

A. Barry Goldwater Air Force Range.

——— ?¿ ———

Q. What Arizona river begins in Mexico and flows northward?

A. San Pedro.

——— ?¿ ———

Q. What Arizona river seems to begin in Mexico, but actually rises in Arizona and loops through Mexico?

A. Santa Cruz.

——— ?¿ ———

Q. Where is the Arizona Temple of the Church of Jesus Christ of Latter-day Saints (Mormon)?

A. Mesa.

——— ?¿ ———

Q. What famous U.S. highway, bypassed by interstate 40, is preserved as a historic route in northwestern Arizona?

A. U.S. Route 66.

——— ?¿ ———

Q. What national monument was originally a fortified Mormon ranch?

A. Pipe Spring National Monument.

Geography

Q. What Coconino County volcano was active less than 1,000 years ago?

A. Sunset Crater.

—————?¿—————

Q. Where is the only point in the nation common to four states?

A. Four Corners.

—————?¿—————

Q. What county was taken away by Congress in 1866 to form the southern tip of Nevada?

A. Pah-Ute.

—————?¿—————

Q. An endowment to the University of Arizona in 1985 consisted of what ghost town?

A. Total Wreck.

—————?¿—————

Q. What was the name of the long-time Spanish and Mexican outpost near today's planned city of Rio Rico?

A. Calabasas.

—————?¿—————

Q. Sun City deed restrictions allow residents' children under 18 to reside there how long?

A. Ninety days.

—————?¿—————

Q. How many people live in the original Sun City?

A. 46,000.

—————?¿—————

Q. How many dams are on the Colorado River along Arizona's borders?

Geography

A. Seven.

———— ?ᒻ ————

Q. What World War II Army installation is still active in southwestern Arizona?

A. Yuma Proving Ground.

———— ?ᒻ ————

Q. Where is Totem Pole Rock?

A. Monument Valley.

———— ?ᒻ ————

Q. How many shuffleboard courts are in Sun City?

A. 72.

———— ?ᒻ ————

Q. What planned community occupies a World War II recreation site for Army flying cadets, known as Site Six?

A. Lake Havasu City.

———— ?ᒻ ————

Q. To the nearest thousand, how many aircraft were registered in Arizona in 1988?

A. 6,000.

———— ?ᒻ ————

Q. What 1,000-year-old Hopi pueblo is perhaps the oldest continuously-inhabited community in North America?

A. Oraibi.

———— ?ᒻ ————

Q. What is the average age of Sun City residents?

A. 71.2 years.

Geography

Q. The rose garden at Glendale's Saguaro Ranch Park is popular for what spring ceremonies?

A. Weddings.

———?¿———

Q. What town established in 1752 is the oldest European town in Arizona?

A. Tubac.

———?¿———

Q. What city was founded in 1775, the year the American revolution began?

A. Tucson.

———?¿———

Q. What 12,633-foot peak is the highest point in Arizona?

A. Humphreys Peak.

———?¿———

Q. Humphreys Peak is the tallest of the San Francisco Peaks; what is the second-tallest at 12,356 feet?

A. Aggasiz peak.

———?¿———

Q. How high is Arizona's lowest point at the Mexican border south of Yuma?

A. Seventy feet.

———?¿———

Q. How many "life zones" are represented between Yuma and the top of Humphreys peak?

A. Six.

———?¿———

Q. What is Arizona's official state flower?

Geography

A. The saguaro cactus bloom.

———— ?¿ ————

Q. What is Arizona's official state tree?

A. The paloverde.

———— ?¿ ————

Q. What is Arizona's official state bird?

A. The cactus wren.

———— ?¿ ————

Q. What is Arizona's official neckwear, by proclamation of the Legislature?

A. The bola tie.

———— ?¿ ————

Q. What is Arizona's official state mammal?

A. The ring-tailed cat.

———— ?¿ ————

Q. What rural post office has moved 15 miles since 1977, confusing travelers and mapmakers?

A. Happy Jack, AZ 86024.

———— ?¿ ————

Q. What feature of Wupatki ruin makes experts think it was influenced by visitors from Mexico?

A. A ball court.

———— ?¿ ————

Q. What is the name of the scenic creek that joins the Colorado River at Lees Ferry?

A. Paria.

Geography

Q. What Phoenix thoroughfare was patterned after a counterpart in Fresno, California?

A. Grand Avenue.

―――――?¿―――――

Q. What scenic railroad uses tracks first laid to build a levee along the Colorado River?

A. Yuma Valley Railroad.

―――――?¿―――――

Q. What river joins the Agua Fria at Sun City?

A. New River.

―――――?¿―――――

Q. What Maricopa County recreation site utilizes a pit dug to obtain roadbuilding material?

A. Firebird Lake.

―――――?¿―――――

Q. What is Arizona's third-busiest airport, behind Phoenix and Tucson?

A. Grand Canyon.

―――――?¿―――――

Q. What "beauty resort" has lured wealthy women to the Phoenix area since the 1940s?

A. Elizabeth Arden's Maine Chance.

―――――?¿―――――

Q. Where is the Museum of the Horse?

A. Patagonia.

―――――?¿―――――

Q. What is the total projected length of Central Arizona Project viaducts?

A. 335 miles.

———— ?¿ ————

Q. Mount Baldy, at 11,590 feet, is the tallest in what mountain range?

A. White Mountains.

———— ?¿ ————

Q. Eastern Arizona College, one of Arizona's oldest junior colleges, is in what Graham County town?

A. Thatcher.

———— ?¿ ————

Q. What Phoenix suburb became an incorporated city in 1989, with 3,000 residents and one employee?

A. Queen Creek.

———— ?¿ ————

Q. What was the site of Arizona's first state park?

A. Tubac Presidio State Historic Park.

———— ?¿ ————

Q. Goldwater's, a department store chain begun in Prescott and Phoenix, is now part of what national chain?

A. Robinson's.

———— ?¿ ————

Q. What is the common name for stripes down the faces of northern Arizona's sandstone cliffs, made by washed-down minerals?

A. "Desert varnish."

———— ?¿ ————

Q. What parallel of latitude did early explorers follow in search of transportation routes across northern Arizona?

A. 35th.

————?¿————

Q. What was the tallest building in Arizona as of 1990?

A. The 40-story Valley Bank Center, Phoenix.

————?¿————

Q. Besides celebrating July 4 and Cinco de Mayo, some Arizona Hispanics celebrate Mexican Independence Day when?

A. September 16.

————?¿————

Q. What Arizona county seat enjoys three courthouses from three different eras?

A. Florence, Pinal County.

————?¿————

Q. What Arizona town, scene of the Pleasant Valley War, still is not reached by paved highway?

A. Young.

————?¿————

Q. What airline established in Phoenix in 1983 quickly grew to a major U.S. airline?

A. America West.

————?¿————

Q. What type of Mexican export creates heavy truck and rail traffic through Nogales, Arizona?

A. Produce.

————?¿————

Q. What state park near Apache Junction celebrates Arizona's foremost legend?

A. Lost Dutchman State Park.

Q. What 1925 dam created Canyon Lake on the Salt River?

A. Mormon Flat.

———— ?ι ————

Q. What Salt River lake is formed by Horse Mesa Dam?

A. Apache.

———— ?ι ————

Q. Bartlett Dam and Bartlett Lake are on what river?

A. Verde.

———— ?ι ————

Q. What town south of Tucson began in 1966 as a planned community?

A. Green Valley.

———— ?ι ————

Q. What scenic town lies in two counties?

A. Sedona.

———— ?ι ————

Q. What frontier fort critical to Arizona development was actually in California?

A. Fort Yuma.

———— ?ι ————

Q. What wealthy town is sandwiched between Phoenix and Scottsdale?

A. Paradise Valley.

———— ?ι ————

Q. Where did Phoenix promoters try to emulate the Hollywood bowl in the 1920s?

Geography

A. Echo Canyon Bowl.

————?¿————

Q. Parts of what 1927 resort were included in the classy Phoenician Resort in the 1980s?

A. Jokake Inn.

————?¿————

Q. What flood-prone wash has Scottsdale turned into a green-belt asset?

A. Indian Bend Wash.

————?¿————

Q. What defunct White Mountain logging town frequently reported the nation's coldest temperatures?

A. Maverick.

————?¿————

Q. Painted Rocks State Park is named for what "paintings?"

A. Prehistoric petroglyphs.

————?¿————

Q. What usually-dry river runs past downtown Tucson on its way north to the Gila?

A. Santa Cruz.

————?¿————

Q. What major tributary to Salt River drains much of central Arizona?

A. Verde River.

————?¿————

Q. In what year did Colorado River water first reach Phoenix via the Central Arizona Project?

A. 1985.

Geography

Q. What rock spire is supposedly a clue to whereabouts of the Lost Dutchman Mine?

A. Weavers Needle.

———— *?ι* ————

Q. What distinctive feature in Oak Creek Canyon is now an Arizona state park?

A. Slide Rock.

———— *?ι* ————

Q. Glendale Avenue, a major west Phoenix thoroughfare becomes what upscale street as it goes eastward?

A. Lincoln Drive.

———— *?ι* ————

Q. Pristine Aravaipa Canyon cuts entirely through what southern Arizona mountain range?

A. The Galiuros.

———— *?ι* ————

Q. What is the name of the notorious grade on the Apache Trail?

A. Fish Creek Hill.

———— *?ι* ————

Q. What twisting grade northwest of Phoenix bedeviled truckers until a new up-bound road was built in the 1970s?

A. Yarnell Hill.

———— *?ι* ————

Q. Bobby Troup's lyrics for the pop song "Route 66" urged travelers "don't forget" what dot on the Arizona map?

A. Winona.

Geography

Q. The Santa Fe, Prescott & Phoenix Railroad was so crooked that Santa Fe engineers still call it what?

A. The Peavine.

———?¿———

Q. What is the name of the "Harvey House" in Williams, recently refurbished as a depot and museum complex?

A. Fray Marcos de Niza.

———?¿———

Q. What was the name of the Fred Harvey hotel and restaurant in Winslow, a magnet to early travelers?

A. La Posada.

———?¿———

Q. What is the name of the prominence at Flagstaff's western edge where Lowell Observatory is located?

A. Mars Hill.

———?¿———

Q. What are the two former names of 27th Avenue in Phoenix?

A. Mission Drive, Lateral 14.

———?¿———

Q. What were the "laterals" which lent their names and numbers to north-south thoroughfares in the Salt River Valley?

A. Irrigation ditches.

———?¿———

Q. Arizona has only three highway tunnels. Where is the longest one, 1,433 feet?

A. Mule Pass, near Bisbee.

Geography

Q. What Tucson district contains about 150 examples of adobe architecture?

A. Barrio Historico.

——— ?¿ ———

Q. What Tucson barrio was named for its *laissez-faire,* anything goes reputation?

A. Barrio Libre.

——— ?¿ ———

Q. What Phoenix suburb was founded in 1892 as a Dunkard temperance colony?

A. Glendale.

——— ?¿ ———

Q. What mile-square municipality is completely contained within another municipality?

A. South Tucson.

——— ?¿ ———

Q. What is the common name for whitish soil deposits which form a "hardpan" in desert soil?

A. Caliche.

——— ?¿ ———

Q. What Apache county formation has one of Arizona's best petroglyph displays?

A. Newspaper Rock.

——— ?¿ ———

Q. The two geographic names spelled out in Arizona statutes are the Mogollon Rim and _____.

A. Hoover Dam.

Geography

Q. What is the name of the hill where Jerome is located?

A. Cleopatra Hill.

———————?¿———————

Q. What is the name of the most-photographed viewpoint on the Mogollon Rim?

A. Hi View.

———————?¿———————

Q. What modern railroad, completed in 1973, operates entirely in Arizona and connects with no other?

A. The Black Mesa & Lake Powell Railroad.

———————?¿———————

Q. What former spa can no longer be reached by automobile?

A. Verde Hot Springs.

———————?¿———————

Q. Arizona's geographic center lies in what colorfully-named area north of Phoenix?

A. Bloody Basin.

———————?¿———————

Q. What historic trading post is near the junction of the Colorado and Little Colorado rivers?

A. Cameron.

———————?¿———————

Q. Bell Rock and Coffee Pot are located near the mouth of what canyon?

A. Oak Creek.

Geography

Q. What was the last name of Sedona, the woman for whom the colorful town was named?

A. Schnebly.

———— ?¿ ————

Q. What color is used in the names of a coal-bearing mesa, a river and a central Arizona canyon?

A. Black.

———— ?¿ ————

Q. What is the year-ground temperature inside Colossal Cave east of Tucson?

A. 72 degrees.

———— ?¿ ————

Q. What 1893 Tucson museum shows prehistoric and historic man in relationship to Southwestern environments?

A. Arizona State Museum.

———— ?¿ ————

Q. What foundation operates a venerable archaeological museum near Texas Canyon, 64 miles east of Tucson?

A. Amerind Foundation.

———— ?¿ ————

Q. What is Arizona's largest community college?

A. Pima Community College.

———— ?¿ ————

Q. East Clear Creek flows into the Little Colorado River; where does West Clear Creek go?

A. The Verde River.

Geography

Q. What lake claims 1,900 miles of shoreline in two states?

A. Lake Powell.

————?¿————

Q. What is the common name for the basaltic rock found throughout northern Arizona?

A. Malapais.

————?¿————

Q. According to a 1990 study, Arizona has the largest number of what kind of visitors in comparison to other states?

A. Winter visitors.

————?¿————

Q. In what town are the restored Bird Cage Theater, Crystal Palace and Fly's photo studio?

A. Tombstone.

————?¿————

Q. What late-August festival has helped celebrate Tucson's founding for more than 200 years?

A. La Fiesta De San Augustin.

————?¿————

Q. Writers use what name to describe southern Arizona's free-standing mountains--the Catalinas, Huachucas, etc.?

A. "Sky islands."

————?¿————

Q. The Pima Air Museum, world's largest privately-financed historic aircraft collection, is near what city?

A. Tucson.

Geography

Q. The former residence of Territorial Gov. John C. Fremont is one of the oldest adobe houses in what city?

A. Tucson.

———— ?ᴢ ————

Q. Where is the world's largest Lady Banksia rose tree, planted in 1885?

A. Tombstone.

———— ?ᴢ ————

Q. What town turned a former prison into a high school, giving subsequent athletic teams the nickname "Criminals"?

A. Yuma.

———— ?ᴢ ————

Q. "The Mittens" are a rock spire in what natural wonder?

A. Monument Valley.

———— ?ᴢ ————

Q. Who were the pioneer traders who welcomed early tourists to Monument Valley?

A. Harry and "Mike" Goulding.

———— ?ᴢ ————

Q. Where is the nation's most productive open-pit copper mine?

A. Morenci.

———— ?ᴢ ————

Q. Which Arizona county led in citrus production during the 1980s?

A. Yuma.

Geography

Q. What is the population density of La Paz County, most sparsely-populated area of the state?

A. 3.3 people per square mile.

————?¿————

Q. What is the population density of Maricopa County?

A. 225 people per square mile.

————?¿————

Q. What downtown Tucson shrine is dedicated to any of several unredeemed sinners of local legend?

A. El Tiradito (The Castaway).

————?¿————

Q. What county courthouse has a dome of mosaic tile?

A. Pima County.

————?¿————

Q. What Spanish word describes a hut built of vertical stakes driven in the ground with mud between them?

A. *Jacal.*

————?¿————

Q. Where is the Miners' Monument, also called "Iron Man," formed of molten copper over a concrete core?

A. Bisbee.

————?¿————

Q. What is the name of the slope where the Cochise County Courthouse and Miners' Monument are located?

A. Quality Hill.

Geography

Q. What Phoenix museum displays a collection of firefighting equipment?

A. The Hall of Flame.

———— ?¿ ————

Q. Tucson is popular with astronomers, but what University of Arizona facility has the public seeing stars?

A. Flandreau Planetarium.

———— ?¿ ————

Q. What is the name of the Scottsdale city park devoted to the iron horse?

A. McCormick Railroad Park.

———— ?¿ ————

Q. What southern Arizona town uses a historic railroad depot for town and county offices?

A. Patagonia.

———— ?¿ ————

Q. Glen Canyon Dam was begun in 1956. When was it completed?

A. 1966.

———— ?¿ ————

Q. How high does Glen Canyon Dam rise above the Colorado River?

A. 575 feet.

———— ?¿ ————

Q. America's second-highest steel arch bridge rises 618 feet above what canyon floor?

A. Glen Canyon.

Geography

Q. The seal of which Arizona county features the head of a Hereford bull?

A. Apache.

———?¿———

Q. Arizona is divided into how many counties?

A. 15.

———?¿———

Q. What Hohokam Indian site is a city park in east Phoenix?

A. Pueblo Grande.

———?¿———

Q. What southern Arizona village, founded by dissident Mormons, is now site of a Benedictine monastery?

A. St. David.

———?¿———

Q. In what mountain town is the Shrine of St. Joseph located?

A. Yarnell.

———?¿———

Q. Where was the hydroelectric generating station named a historic landmark by the American Society of Mechanial Engineers?

A. Childs.

———?¿———

Q. Interstate 15 sweeps through what spectacular canyon in northwestern Arizona?

A. The Virgin River Gorge.

Q. How many stripes or "rays" are on the Arizona state flag?

A. Thirteen.

———— ?¿ ————

Q. How wide is Arizona at its widest point?

A. 338 miles.

———— ?¿ ————

Q. What former gold mining town now features burros roaming the streets?

A. Oatman.

———— ?¿ ————

Q. What color is the star in the center of the Arizona flag?

A. Copper.

———— ?¿ ————

Q. What is the name of the World War II flying school that became Mesa's municipal airport?

A. Falcon Field.

———— ?¿ ————

Q. What Mesa institution displays a fine collection of warplanes?

A. Champlin Fighter Museum.

———— ?¿ ————

Q. Waters north of the Mogollon Rim flow generally in what direction?

A. North.

———— ?¿ ————

Q. Where is Arizona's only covered bridge located?

Geography

A. Near Airipine.

————?¿————

Q. What expensive interstate highway passes through Arizona but reaches no major towns in the state?

A. I-15.

————?¿————

Q. What semi-precious stone is frequently a by product of copper mines?

A. Turquoise.

————?¿————

Q. Alpine is one Arizona community at 8,000 feet elevation. Name another one.

A. Summerhaven.

————?¿————

Q. Part of London Bridge was shipped stone-by-stone and reconstructed at what Arizona city?

A. Lake Havasu City.

————?¿————

Q. Where is the New Cornelia open pit mine located?

A. Ajo.

————?¿————

Q. The Tucson, Cornelia & Gila Bend Railroad did not go to what city?

A. Tucson.

————?¿————

Q. What railroad connected the lumber mills of the White Mountains with the Santa Fe mainline?

A. Apache Railway.

Geography

Q. Where is Arizona's only paper mill?

A. Snowflake.

———— ?¿ ————

Q. What sort of weaponry is commemorated at an underground museum south of Tucson?

A. Titan II missiles.

———— ?¿ ————

Q. What was the original name of the World War II flying school that became the American Graduate School of International Management?

A. Thunderbird I.

———— ?¿ ————

Q. The dwindling percentage of actual copper in ore from Arizona's mines is down to what figure?

A. 60 per cent.

———— ?¿ ————

Q. What was an early name for the White Mountains?

A. Black Mesa.

———— ?¿ ————

Q. Zane Grey Lodge and Kohls Ranch resort are on what creek?

A. Tonto Creek.

———— ?¿ ————

Q. What is the highest point on the Mogollon Rim at 8,074 feet?

A. Baker Butte.

———— ?¿ ————

Q. What is the name of the partially restored Catholic mission now a national monument?

A. Tumacacori.

————?¿————

Q. What downtown Phoenix park was rebuilt in the 1980s to include underground parking and a controversial above-ground design?

A. Patriots Square.

————?¿————

Q. What is another name for Willcox Dry Lake?

A. Willcox Playa.

————?¿————

Q. What creek was named for a mountain man who died after eating poisonous plants?

A. Chevelon.

————?¿————

Q. On the average, how high does the Mogollon Rim rise above settlements below?

A. 2,000 feet.

————?¿————

Q. What feature on the Mogollon Rim is named for a pioneer dairy farm?

A. Milk Ranch Point.

————?¿————

Q. What's the name of a popular Prescott-area recreation lake surrounded by granite boulders?

A. Granite Dells.

————?¿————

Q. What has been Arizona's principal farm crop for much of the 20th century?

A. Cotton.

Geography

Q. When did the government establish "forest preserves," now national forests?

A. 1898.

———— ?ι ————

Q. What Arizona community claims the world's largest sundial?

A. Carefree.

———— ?ι ————

Q. What planned community claims the world's tallest fountain at 560 feet?

A. Fountain Hills.

———— ?ι ————

Q. The anchor of what battleship, sunk at Pearl Harbor, is displayed near the Arizona Capitol?

A. The U.S.S. Arizona.

———— ?ι ————

Q. Of what material is the dome of the 1901 state Capitol?

A. Copper.

———— ?ι ————

Q. Where in the Prescott area did wealthy Phoenix residents establish summer homes beginning in 1900?

A. Iron Springs.

——— ?ι ————

Q. About what proportion of Arizonans are native-born?

A. One-third.

Geography

Q. What state contributes the most newcomers to Arizona each year?

A. California.

―――――?¿―――――

Q. What state contributes the largest number of new, permanent residents to Arizona?

A. Michigan.

―――――?¿―――――

Q. What prestigious, five-star resort west of Phoenix was sold in 1990 to a Japanese firm?

A. The Wigwam.

―――――?¿―――――

Q. What Maricopa County towns owe their existence to an Akron-based manufacturing company—and two world wars?

A. Goodyear and Litchfield Park.

―――――?¿―――――

Q. What county is 64 percent national forest?

A. Greenlee.

―――――?¿―――――

Q. What prominence in Tombstone Canyon is a Bisbee landmark?

A. Castle Rock.

―――――?¿―――――

Q. Warren and Lowell are burroughs of what city?

A. Bisbee.

―――――?¿―――――

Q. How many passengers used Phoenix Sky Harbor Airport in 1989?

Geography

A. 20.7 million.

—————— ?¿ ——————

Q. What natural wonder in southeastern Arizona was kept secret 14 years after its 1974 discovery to protect it?

A. Karchner Caverns State Park.

—————— ?¿ ——————

Q. A plank road across sand dunes west of Yuma was built in 1915 to link Arizona roads with what city?

A. San Diego.

—————— ?¿ ——————

Q. Some people go to Tucson each February to get stoned at the world's largest exposition of its kind. What is it?

A. The Tucson Gem and Mineral Show.

—————— ?¿ ——————

Q. Name the unlikely desert junction that swells to a metropolis in winter with rockhounds and sun worshippers.

A. Quartzsite.

—————— ?¿ ——————

Q. Name the natural arch, long privately-owned, that finally became an Arizona state park.

A. Tonto Natural Bridge.

—————— ?¿ ——————

Q. What is the common name of the escarpment that runs diagonally across Arizona but is most visible above Payson?

A. The Mogollon Rim.

Geography

Q. What is the name of the tableland that slopes northeast from the Mogollon escarpment to Four Corners?

A. The Colorado Plateau.

―――――?¿――――

Q. What is the better-known name for twisting, scenic Arizona Route 88 between Apache Junction and Roosevelt?

A. The Apache Trail.

―――――?¿――――

Q. Where are Punch and Judy and other denizens of the "Wonderland of Rocks" found?

A. Chiricahua National Monument.

―――――?¿――――

Q. A stone pyramid on the desert commemorates the World War II training of the 81st Infantry Division at what post?

A. Camp Horn.

―――――?¿――――

Q. The Colorado River empties into what body of water?

A. The Gulf of California.

―――――?¿――――

Q. About how much of the nation's copper is produced in Arizona?

A. 60 percent.

―――――?¿――――

Q. What imaginary line, used in most Arizona land surveys, lent its name to Baseline Road?

A. The Gila and Salt River Base Line.

Geography

Q. The "point of beginning" for Arizona land surveys is near the confluence of what two rivers?

A. The Salt and the Gila.

———— ?¿ ————

Q. What percentage of Arizona is federally owned?

A. 70 percent.

———— ?¿ ————

Q. What is the Arizona state gem?

A. Turquoise.

———— ?¿ ————

Q. What are the Arizona state colors?

A. Blue and gold.

———— ?¿ ————

Q. Would you believe Arizona has an official state reptile? What is it?

A. The ridge-nosed rattlesnake.

———— ?¿ ————

Q. If Arizona's mountains were flattened, the state might be as broad as Texas. What is its average elevation?

A. 4,000 feet.

———— ?¿ ————

Q. Arizona's 1990 population was about how many times as large as its population at the beginning of World War II?

A. Seven times.

———— ?¿ ————

Q. The number of square miles covered by Phoenix, 17 in 1950, grew to how many by 1990?

Geography

A. 404.

—————?¿—————

Q. What was the Phoenix area's first major shopping mall, opened in 1957?

A. Park Central.

—————?¿—————

Q. What year did Chris-Town, Arizona's first enclosed shopping mall, open?

A. 1961.

—————?¿—————

Q. What gemstone, mined on the San Carlos Reservation, has given its name to a community there?

A. Peridot.

—————?¿—————

Q. During the 1970s and '80s Arizona cities bought rural ranches for what purpose?

A. Water rights.

—————?¿—————

Q. What national forest consists of a dozen unconnected "islands" of forest in southern Arizona?

A. Coronado.

—————?¿—————

Q. In what census year did Phoenix surpass Tucson as the largest city in Arizona?

A. 1920.

—————?¿—————

Q. What modern city calls itself "The Old Pueblo"?

A. Tucson.

Geography

Q. What artificial lake, dammed in 1956, helped put the White Mountain Apaches in the tourist business?

A. Hawley Lake.

——— ?¿ ———

Q. What popular ski resort is a White Mountain Apache tribal enterprise?

A. Sunrise.

——— ?¿ ———

Q. What route did the State Transportation Board name Arizona's first historic route in 1986?

A. Arizona 88, The Apache Trail.

——— ?¿ ———

Q. What spectacular canyon's name means "among the cliffs" in Navajo?

A. Canyon de Chelly.

——— ?¿ ———

Q. What is Canyon de Chelly's colorful chief tributary?

A. Canyon del Muerto.

——— ?¿ ———

Q. What spire in Canyon de Chelly is taller than the Washington Monument?

A. Spider Rock.

——— ?¿ ———

Q. What Mexico-to-Canada highway passes through Arizona?

A. U.S. 89.

——— ?¿ ———

Q. What very short Interstate highway leads Arizona travelers to Mexico?

Geography

A. I-19.

———?¿———

Q. Name the two towns that vanished when Ray Mines Division of Kennecott expanded its pit in the 1960s.

A. Ray and Sonora.

———?¿———

Q. What is the common name for bands of brightly colored sand and volcanic material across northern Arizona?

A. Painted Desert.

———?¿———

Q. What lake was formed when the hooves of dairy cattle compacted what had been a mere meadow?

A. Mormon Lake.

———?¿———

Q. What lake was created in the 1960s to trade water from one watershed to another?

A. Blue Ridge Reservoir.

———?¿———

Q. What former Arizona county seat lies beneath the waters of Lake Mead?

A. Callville, seat of Pah-Ute County.

———?¿———

Q. U.S. 89 between Florence and Oracle is also known as what?

A. Pinal Pioneer Parkway.

———?¿———

Q. What series of multi-colored cliffs repeats itself along U.S. 89 north of Flagstaff?

Geography

A. Echo Cliffs.

———— ?¿ ————

Q. What two adjoining municipalities occupy Round Valley?

A. Springerville and Eagar.

———— ?¿ ————

Q. What is the common name of U.S. 666 along Arizona's eastern border?

A. The Coronado Trail.

———— ?¿ ————

Q. What intermittent waterfall on the Little Colorado River is taller than Niagara Falls?

A. Grand Falls.

———— ?¿ ————

Q. What is the chronological order of Arizona's admission to the Union?

A. It was the 48th state.

———— ?¿ ————

Q. What was the last state admitted to the Union before Arizona?

A. New Mexico.

———— ?¿ ————

Q. Most of Arizona's land is publicly owned. How much is in private hands?

A. 16 to 17 percent.

———— ?¿ ————

Q. Which transcontinental railroad parallels Interstate 40 across northern Arizona?

A. Atchison, Topeka & Santa Fe.

Geography

Q. What is the name of the lake impounded by Hoover Dam?

A. Lake Mead.

———————?¿———————

Q. Magnificient Lake Powell was impounded by the construction of what dam?

A. Glen Canyon Dam.

———————?¿———————

Q. Lake Powell lies mostly in what state?

A. Utah.

———————?¿———————

Q. What natural arch was made more accessible by Lake Powell?

A. Rainbow Bridge.

———————?¿———————

Q. What historic river crossing was covered by Lake Powell?

A. Crossing of the Fathers.

———————?¿———————

Q. The motto on Arizona's state seal is Ditat Deus. What does it mean?

A. God enriches.

———————?¿———————

Q. Who built Arizona's first extensive irrigation project?

A. The Hohokam, whose culture "vanished" in the 1400s.

———————?¿———————

Q. What was the keystone of the nation's first multi-purpose reclamation project?

Geography

A. Roosevelt Dam.

———— ?¿ ————

Q. What is the largest lake entirely within Arizona's borders?

A. Roosevelt Lake.

———— ?¿ ————

Q. The San Francisco River is a tributary to what river system?

A. The Gila.

———— ?¿ ————

Q. What Phoenix preserve is the largest municipal park in the world?

A. Phoenix South Mountain Park.

———— ?¿ ————

Q. What animal-shaped peak is a major Phoenix landmark?

A. Camelback Mountain.

———— ?¿ ————

Q. The post office at Marinette was renamed for what retirement community in 1958?

A. Youngtown.

———— ?¿ ————

Q. Four Peaks is in what national forest?

A. Tonto.

———— ?¿ ————

Q. What digit-shaped outcropping rises on Prescott's west horizon?

A. Thumb Butte.

THE GRAND CANYON

C H A P T E R   T W O

Q. Before the Grand Canyon became a protected natural attraction, who were its users and developers?

A. Miners.

———————?¿———————

Q. Grand Canyon National Park attracts in excess of how many visitors per year?

A. 4.2 million.

———————?¿———————

Q. By air it is about 12 miles from South Rim to North Rim. How far is it by highway?

A. 219 miles.

———————?¿———————

Q. What is the difference in elevation between the South Rim and the higher North Rim?

A. 1,324 feet.

———————?¿———————

Q. Vertically, how much lower is Phantom Ranch than Grand Canyon Village?

A. 4,376 feet.

The Grand Canyon

Q. When was Grand Canyon National Park established?

A. February 26, 1919.

———— ?¿ ————

Q. What is the only guest facility inside the Grand Canyon?

A. Phantom Ranch.

———— ?¿ ————

Q. Who was an early Grand Canyon developer who later became a Congressman and U.S. Senator?

A. Ralph Cameron.

———— ?¿ ————

Q. What is the name of the popular oasis 3,200 feet below the South Rim on Bright Angel Trail?

A. Indian Gardens.

———— ?¿ ————

Q. What popular form of transportation has carried millions of tourists down Bright Angel Trail?

A. Mules.

Q. What year was the suspension bridge built across the Colorado River near Phantom Ranch?

A. 1928.

———— ?¿ ————

Q. What is the name of the series of switchbacks three miles down Bright Angel Trail?

A. Jacobs Ladder.

The Grand Canyon

Q. Who is the famous painter of the Grand Canyon whose bold paintings hang in the National Museum of American Art?

A. Thomas Moran.

————?¿————

Q. Which of Grand Canyon's several trails crosses the canyon from rim to rim?

A. Kaibab.

————?¿————

Q. For whom was Kibbey Butte named?

A. Joseph H. Kibbey, Arizona territorial judge and governor.

————?¿————

Q. What year did Scenic Airways of Phoenix begin tourist flights over the Grand Canyon?

A. 1928.

————?¿————

Q. Where on the South Rim does a distinctive tower of native stone stand guard?

A. Desert View.

————?¿————

Q. The Grand Canyon railroad depot, finished in 1905, is made of what?

A. Logs.

————?¿————

Q. On which rim of the Grand Canyon is Cape Royal?

A. North Rim.

The Grand Canyon

Q. Who was the Spanish captain who never visited Grand Canyon, but gave his name to a location and a hotel?

A. Pedro de Tovar.

———— ?¿ ————

Q. What Arizona governor narrated 25 annual NBC broadcasts of Easter sunrise at Grand Canyon?

A. J. Howard Pyle.

———— ?¿ ————

Q. What Grand Canyon tributary is often called "Arizona's Shangri-La?"

A. Havasu Canyon.

———— ?¿ ————

Q. Which is the tallest of five waterfalls in Havasu Canyon?

A. Mooney (200-plus feet).

———— ?¿ ————

Q. What is the name of the village in Havasu Canyon that can only be reached by trail?

A. Supai.

———— ?¿ ————

Q. The volcanic formation Vulcan's Throne overlooks what rapids?

A. Lava Falls.

———— ?¿ ————

Q. What national forest brackets Grand Canyon National Forest on the north and south?

A. Kaibab.

The Grand Canyon

Q. What is the name of the isolated plateau that includes the north rim of Grand Canyon?

A. Kaibab Plateau.

———?¿———

Q. Two species of animal peculiar to the Kaibab Plateau include the Kaibab mule deer and Kaibab what?

A. Squirrel.

———?¿———

Q. How long is greater Grand Canyon, including Marble Canyon on the east and Boulder Canyon on the west?

A. 280 miles.

———?¿———

Q. Who was the Grand Canyon hiker who wrote the 1967 book *The Man Who Walked Through Time*?

A. Colin Fletcher.

———?¿———

Q. What is the name of the massive limestone formation at the top of the Grand Canyon's inner gorge?

A. Redwall.

———?¿———

Q. How old is Vishnu Schist, an ancient rock found in the Grand Canyon?

A. 2.2 billion years.

———?¿———

Q. What year did composer Ferde Grofe's "Grand Canyon Suite" premier?

A. 1932.

The Grand Canyon

Q. What is the name of the most-used trail into Grand Canyon?

A. Bright Angel.

———— ?ι ————

Q. Which Spanish lieutenant led the first Europeans to see the Grand Canyon in 1540?

A. Garcia Lopez de Cardenas.

———— ?ι ————

Q. What kind of creature was the fictional *Brighty Of The Grand Canyon*?

A. A burro.

———— ?ι ————

Q. What Grand Canyon feature's name is a 19th-century slang term meaning "knock-out blow" or "finisher"?

A. Sockdolager Rapids.

———— ?ι ————

Q. Missing rock strata from "The Great Unconformity" in Grand Canyon represent how many years?

A. 1.2 billion.

———— ?ι ————

Q. What plateau below Grand Canyon Village separates the upper and inner gorges?

A. Tonto Plateau.

———— ?ι ————

Q. What transportation system was reopened in 1989, offering tourists another way to visit the Grand Canyon?

A. The Grand Canyon Railway.

The Grand Canyon

Q. What is the major feature of Tuweep Unit of Grand Canyon National Park?

A. Toroweap Cliffs.

—————?¿—————

Q. What Grand Canyon feature is named for the first Spaniard to explore the Colorado River in 1540?

A. Alarcon Terrace.

—————?¿—————

Q. Who was the early Canyon entrepreneur whose name was given to a trail and his former tourist camp?

A. William Wallace Bass.

—————?¿—————

Q. From what town does the Grand Canyon Railway begin its trip to South Rim Village?

A. Williams.

—————?¿—————

Q. What was the name of the first hotel at Grand Canyon, built in 1904?

A. Grand View.

—————?¿—————

Q. Who lost an index finger in an accident and later told tourists he wore it off pointing out Grand Canyon sights?

A. John "Cap" Hance.

—————?¿—————

Q. Canyon formations called "temples" are named for what three Hindu dieties?

A. Brahma, Shiva and Vishnu.

The Grand Canyon

Q. Who said of Grand Canyon, "Leave it as it is; you cannot improve on it; not a bit."?

A. Theodore Roosevelt.

———— ?¿ ————

Q. Culinary water for both rims is pumped from where on the North Kaibab Trail?

A. Roaring Springs.

———— ?¿ ————

Q. How many major rapids are within Grand Canyon?

A. 75.

———— ?¿ ————

Q. Thousands of people now "run" the Colorado River by boat each year; how many made the trip between 1867 and 1948?

A. A total of 96.

———— ?¿ ————

Q. What is the average width of the Colorado River through Grand Canyon?

A. 300 feet.

———— ?¿ ————

Q. What part of the year is the North Rim open to visitors?

A. Mid-May to Mid-October.

———— ?¿ ————

Q. What are the names of the venerable Fred Harvey lodges at the South Rim?

A. El Tovar and Bright Angel.

HISTORY

CHAPTER THREE

Q. Phoenix was founded on ruins left by what vanished group of farmers?
A. The Hohokam.

——— ?¿ ———

Q. Who was the first European explorer to enter Arizona in 1539?
A. Fray Marcos de Niza.

——— ?¿ ———

Q. What Spanish explorer led a large expedition through Arizona in 1540, looking for cities of gold?
A. Francisco Vasquez de Coronado.

——— ?¿ ———

Q. What missionary brought Catholicism and cattle ranching to southern Arizona around 1690?
A. Father Eusebio Francisco Kino.

——— ?¿ ———

Q. What Spanish mission is called "The White Dove Of The Desert?"
A. Mission San Xavier del Bac.

——— ?¿ ———

Q. Who was the millionaire owner of the Congress Gold Mine, builder of railroads, brother of a territorial governor?

53

A. Frank M. Murphy.

———— ?¿ ————

Q. What Phoenix streetcar system builder later developed the Pacific Electric system in California?

A. Moses H. Sherman.

———— ?¿ ————

Q. Where was Arizona's first capital in 1864?

A. Prescott.

———— ?¿ ————

Q. What was Arizona's capital city between 1867 and 1877?

A. Tucson.

———— ?¿ ————

Q. When did Phoenix become Arizona's permanent capital?

A. 1889.

———— ?¿ ————

Q. What famous Arizona sheriff and mayor was killed in Cuba during the Spanish-American War?

A. William E. "Buckey" O'Neill.

———— ?¿ ————

Q. When did President Taft sign the bill admitting Arizona to the Union?

A. February 14, 1912.

———— ?¿ ————

Q. In what year was the name of Arizona State College (Tempe) changed to Arizona State University?

A. 1958.

Q. When was Roosevelt Dam dedicated?

A. March 18, 1911.

———— ?¿ ————

Q. What was the name of the adventurer whose ditch company founded Phoenix?

A. Jack Swilling.

———— ?¿ ————

Q. Who was the expatriated Englishman generally credited with naming Phoenix?

A. Darrel Duppa.

———— ?¿ ————

Q. Jack Swilling's original community was near what modern Phoenix landmark?

A. Sky Harbor airport.

———— ?¿ ————

Q. John Y.T. Smith grew what crop on one of the Salt River Valley's first farms in the 1860s?

A. Hay.

———— ?¿ ————

Q. When was the western or downtown Phoenix townsite surveyed?

A. 1870.

———— ?¿ ————

Q. Phoenix legislators foisted the University of Arizona off on Tucson in 1886, preferring what institution?

A. The insane asylum.

———— ?¿ ————

Q. What was the name of the Phoenix area's first resort hotel, opened in 1909?

History

A. Ingleside.

———— ?¿ ————

Q. What remote resort began as a sanitorium, then began luring the rich and famous?

A. Castle Hot Springs.

———— ?¿ ————

Q. What persecuted religious group colonized Arizona in large numbers in the 1870s and '80s?

A. Mormons.

———— ?¿ ————

Q. What five-star resort opened in 1929?

A. The Arizona Biltmore.

———— ?¿ ————

Q. Governor Benjamin B. Moeur sent the Arizona National Guard in 1934 to stop construction of what dam?

A. Parker Dam.

———— ?¿ ————

Q. What was the relationship of Lees Ferry operator Emma French Lee to Mormon fugitivie John Doyle Lee?

A. 17th wife.

———— ?¿ ————

Q. Where did the first railroad enter Arizona in 1877?

A. Yuma.

———— ?¿ ————

Q. What explorer used camels to explore a route across northern Arizona?

A. Edward F. Beale.

Q. A monument at Quartzsite marks the grave of what frontier camel driver?

A. Hadji Ali, or "Hi Jolly."

———— ?¿ ————

Q. What famous American driver won the 1914 road race between Los Angeles and Phoenix?

A. Barney Oldfield.

———— ?¿ ————

Q. What automobile is named for a racer who tested his cars in the Los Angeles-Phoenix road races of 1910 to 1914?

A. Chevrolet.

———— ?¿ ————

Q. In what year did the Uncle Sam become the first steamboat to navigate the Colorado and Gila rivers?

A. 1852.

———— ?¿ ————

Q. What war added much of Arizona to U.S. territory?

A. The Mexican War.

———— ?¿ ————

Q. The northern part of Arizona became U.S. Territory under what treaty?

A. The Treaty of Guadalupe Hidalgo, 1848.

———— ?¿ ————

Q. From 1850 to 1863 Arizona was part of what territory?

A. New Mexico Territory.

———— ?¿ ————

Q. When did Arizona become a separate U.S. territory?

A. February 23, 1863.

History

Q. Besides Spain, Mexico and the U.S., what other "nation" claimed Arizona?

A. The Confederate States of America.

———— ?¿ ————

Q. What is considered the western most "battle" of the U.S. Civil War?

A. The Battle of Picacho Pass.

———— ?¿ ————

Q. How did southern Arizona become part of the United States?

A. The Gadsden Purchase of 1854.

———— ?¿ ————

Q. What river was the U.S.-Mexican boundary from 1850 to 1854?

A. The Gila.

———— ?¿ ————

Q. Who was the pioneer merchant and flour miller who founded Tempe?

A. Charles Trumbull Hayden.

———— ?¿ ————

Q. Who surveyed the 1870 Phoenix townsite and built its first business building?

A. Captain William A. Hancock.

———— ?¿ ————

Q. What Arizona explorer had earlier carried the first news of the California gold rush to Washington?

A. Edward F. Beale.

———— ?¿ ————

Q. Where was the first airport in Phoenix?

A. State Fairgrounds.

———— ?¿ ————

Q. Phoenix' first municipal airport was at Lateral 18 and Christy Road. Where would that be today?

A. 59th Avenue and McDowell.

———— ?¿ ————

Q. What automobile pioneer crossed Arizona in three consecutive years, 1910-12, representing three different auto clubs?

A. A.L. Westgard.

———— ?¿ ————

Q. What well-known bandit is believed to have killed Camp Verde merchants Clint Wingfield and Mack Rodgers in 1899?

A. Thomas "Black Jack" Ketchum.

———— ?¿ ————

Q. What year did steam locomotives haul their last loads on Arizona copper and lumber railroads?

A. 1966.

———— ?¿ ————

Q. What company brought the electronics industry to the Phoenix area in 1956?

A. Motorola.

———— ?¿ ————

Q. The nation's 1965 Christmas postage stamp was first issued from what post office?

A. Silver Bell.

———— ?¿ ————

Q. Remains of sun-worshiper Charles D. Poston were reinterred in 1925 in what sort of crypt?

A. A stone pyramid.

——— ?¿ ———

Q. When was the preserved log schoolhouse at Strawberry built?

A. 1895.

——— ?¿ ———

Q. What president issued a proclamation threatening to use federal troops to control Arizona lawlessness?

A. Chester A. Arthur (1882).

——— ?¿ ———

Q. Arizona's first (and last) governor's mansion was built in 1864 of what material?

A. Logs.

——— ?¿ ———

Q. What famous builder of planned communities began his Arizona career in 1927 hanging doors at the new Westward Ho Hotel?

A. Del E. Webb.

——— ?¿ ———

Q. Since the 1870s, Thirteen-mile Rock has been a milepost 13 miles east of what town?

A. Camp Verde.

——— ?¿ ———

Q. In what year did ice manufacturer S.D. Lount install Phoenix' first telephone from home to factory?

A. 1882.

——— ?¿ ———

Q. The Phoenix landmark known as Tovrea Castle was built to be what?

A. A hotel.

———— ?ι ————

Q. What Phoenix hotel, long the tallest building in town, is now subsidized senior citizen apartments?

A. Westward Ho.

———— ?ι ————

Q. What Indian leader whiled away a quarter of a century in capitivity signing autographs and selling bows and arrows?

A. Geronimo.

———— ?ι ————

Q. Historians identify a $26,000 Army payroll robbery in 1889 by the last name of an officer. What was the name?

A. Wham.

———— ?ι ————

Q. In what vanished town did the Goldwater family establish its first store in 1862?

A. La Paz.

———— ?ι ————

Q. What Phoenix facility is located in a thick-walled adobe building that once housed prisoners of war?

A. Arizona Military Museum.

———— ?ι ————

Q. What year did Phoenix open its first freeway, the Black Canyon (I-17)?

A. 1955.

———— ?ι ————

Q. What year was Interstate 17 completed Phoenix-to-Flagstaff?

A. 1978.

———— ?¿ ————

Q. Missionaries Dominguez and Escalante explored northern Arizona in 1776 while trying to reach what area?

A. San Francisco.

———— ?¿ ————

Q. What was the total number of men who served as Arizona Rangers 1901-1909?

A. 107.

———— ?¿ ————

Q. Who was the former superintendent of the "Hashknife outfit" who became first captain of the Arizona Rangers?

A. Burt Mossman.

———— ?¿ ————

Q. What did the United States pay Mexico for the Gadsden Purchase?

A. $10 million.

———— ?¿ ————

Q. At the peak of the Spanish-Mexican era, about how many Hispanics lived in what would become Arizona?

A. 1,000.

———— ?¿ ————

Q. What narrow-gauge railroad hauled ore from Jerome over a twisting route to Jerome Junction (Chino Valley)?

A. The United Verde & Pacific.

———— ?¿ ————

Q. How did many Mormon "colonizers" earn wages while they established themselves on farms and ranches?

A. Cutting railroad ties.

Q. The original name of the railroad which crossed Arizona 1880-83 was not Santa Fe, but what?

A. Atlantic & Pacific.

———— ?¿ ————

Q. What World War I Prescott Marine was nominated for the Congressional Medal by both the Army and the Navy?

A. John Henry Pruitt.

———— ?¿ ————

Q. What famous Army officer who helped capture Geronimo, later organized Roosevelt's Rough Riders?

A. Leonard Wood.

———— ?¿ ————

Q. Cave Creek was known early in this century for mining and what other industry?

A. Sheep ranching.

———— ?¿ ————

Q. Phoenix Union Station began serving Santa Fe and Southern Pacific passengers in what year?

A. 1923.

———— ?¿ ————

Q. The Apache medicine man Nock-ay-del-klinne stirred up discontent and hostility in what summer?

A. 1881.

———— ?¿ ————

Q. What intrusive 1880s mining camp, now commemorated by a highway marker north of Globe, angered Apaches?

A. McMillanville.

History

Q. What major Phoenix hospital began as a mission to migrants who came seeking help for lung diseases?

A. John C. Lincoln Medical Center.

——— ?¿ ———

Q. When it was completed in 1911, Roosevelt Dam was the world's tallest dam of what kind of construction?

A. Masonry.

——— ?¿ ———

Q. What Arizona city was established in 1957 as a construction town and administrative site for a large dam?

A. Page.

——— ?¿ ———

Q. In what year did Arizona begin registering and regulating motor vehicles?

A. 1913.

——— ?¿ ———

Q. In what year did Phoenix hire its first motorcycle policeman to enforce an 8 mph speed limit?

A. 1910.

——— ?¿ ———

Q. What gold mining community east of Phoenix boomed in 1891, but faded in 1900 when the mines were flooded?

A. Goldfield.

——— ?¿ ———

Q. The treacherous killing of what Apache chief in 1863 set Cochise on a path of vengeance?

A. Mangas Coloradas.

Q. What was the name of the resort hotel opened near Oracle in 1895?

A. The Mountain View.

———— ?¿ ————

Q. How did the Whipple exploration party "light" Christmas trees in a celebration Christmas Eve, 1853?

A. Set fire to a grove of pines.

———— ?¿ ————

Q. The party of what American adventurer is credited with locating gold in the area that was to become Prescott?

A. Joseph H. Walker.

———— ?¿ ————

Q. What mountain man led the Abraham H. Peeples party to what became known as the Weaver mining district?

A. Pauline Weaver.

———— ?¿ ————

Q. Pauline Weaver's first name resulted when Hispanics and Indians mispronounced what original first name?

A. Powell.

———— ?¿ ————

Q. What two scouts led the Mormon battalion through Arizona in 1846?

A. Pauline Weaver and Antoine Leroux.

———— ?¿ ————

Q. What successful Tucson freighter helped put himself out of business by sponsoring pro-railroad legislation?

A. Estevan Ochoa.

Q. Who was the 19-year-old pilot who delivered the first air mail to Tucson in 1915?

A. Katherine Stinson.

———— ?¿ ————

Q. When did transcontinental air mail come to Phoenix and Tucson?

A. 1930.

———— ?¿ ————

Q. Busy Phoenix Sky Harbor airport began in 1928 as the private field of what company?

A. Scenic Airways.

———— ?¿ ————

Q. Where is an 1882 boomtown courthouse preserved?

A. Tombstone Courthouse State Historic Park.

———— ?¿ ————

Q. What living history museum 12 miles north of Phoenix has acquired several of the state's historic buildings?

A. Pioneer Arizona.

———— ?¿ ————

Q. What year was the Cochise County seat moved from Tombstone to Bisbee?

A. 1929.

———— ?¿ ————

Q. Who was the famous sheriff and former Arizona Rangers captain who led the Bisbee Deportation in 1917?

A. Harry Wheeler.

———— ?¿ ————

Q. What famous outlaw is buried in Cochise County, alongside one of Arizona's several Turkey Creeks?

A. Johnny Ringo.

———— ?¿ ————

Q. Who was Wyatt Earp's tubercular sidekick?

A. Doc Holliday.

———— ?¿ ————

Q. Colonel James H. McClintock--printer, Rough Rider, historian, Phoenix postmaster--was a colonel of what?

A. Arizona National Guard.

———— ?¿ ————

Q. Who was the killer and rapist lynched in 1917 because Arizona had abolished capital punishment?

A. Starr Daley.

———— ?¿ ————

Q. What "confirmed" number of German aircraft did Frank Luke Jr. down in his legendary 17 days of combat flying?

A. Fifteen balloons, four airplanes.

———— ?¿ ————

Q. What army surgeon won the first Congressional Medal of Honor for action near Apache Pass in 1861?

A. Bernard J.D. Irwin.

———— ?¿ ————

Q. What was the first railroad to reach Phoenix July 3, 1887?

A. The Maricopa & Phoenix.

———— ?¿ ————

Q. What year did Southern Pacific finally build a mainline into Phoenix?

A. 1926.

History

Q. What famed evangelist appeared in Douglas in 1926, claiming she had been kidnapped to Mexico?

A. Aimee Semple McPherson.

——— ?¿ ———

Q. How did Harriet Fay Southworth, Tex Ritter's future mother-in-law, distinguish herself in 1910?

A. Won a Prescott-Phoenix automobile race.

——— ?¿ ———

Q. E.D. Newcomer, Arizona's first "press photographer," took the state's first aerial photos in what year?

A. 1928.

——— ?¿ ———

Q. General George S. Patton added western Arizona to what California maneuver area early in World War II?

A. The Desert Training Center.

——— ?¿ ———

Q. Secret World War II training at Camp Bouse involved a British experimental light for what kind of vehicle?

A. A tank.

——— ?¿ ———

Q. The manufacturer gave what name to the Concord coach that ran between Tucson and Tombstone?

A. "The Modoc."

——— ?¿ ———

Q. What Tucson booster group was formed to lure tourists and overcome the economic slump after World War I?

A. The Tucson Sunshine Climate Club.

History

Q. What first-rate hotel, opened in 1928, was promoted by Tucson merchants to accomodate winter visitors?

A. El Conquistador.

———— ?¿ ————

Q. Where was Arizona's first sawmill built in 1857?

A. Madera Canyon.

———— ?¿ ————

Q. What was Flagstaff's primary industry from its beginning?

A. Lumbering.

———— ?¿ ————

Q. Who was the chewing gum magnate who built a hilltop mansion on the grounds of the Arizona Biltmore?

A. Phillip Wrigley.

———— ?¿ ————

Q. World War II prison camps for Japanese-Americans were south of Phoenix and where on the Colorado River?

A. Poston.

———— ?¿ ————

Q. What canal, completed in 1887, opened up the desert north and west of Phoenix to farming and settlement?

A. The Arizona Canal.

———— ?¿ ————

Q. Who was the frontier Army officer whose Civil War post in Washington helped him lobby for a separate Territory of Arizona?

A. Major Samuel P. Heintzelman.

———— ?¿ ————

Q. How many people are known to have died in the Pleasant Valley War of the 1880s?

History

A. Thirty.

———— ?¿ ————

Q. Who was the elusive killer who was kidnapped from his native Mexico and hanged at Solomonville in 1902?

A. Augustine Chacon.

———— ?¿ ————

Q. What famous hotel was built three times on the site of today's Sheraton Phoenix?

A. Hotel Adams.

———— ?¿ ————

Q. Name the pioneer Phoenix dwelling, now a museum, noted for its early solar water heating?

A. The Ellis-Shackelford House.

———— ?¿ ————

Q. Where did early residents of Phoenix and Tucson sleep to escape stifling summer heat?

A. In their yards.

———— ?¿ ————

Q. Who was the tough pioneer whose "El Portrero" ranch house near Calabasas was a veritable fortress?

A. Pete Kitchen.

———— ?¿ ————

Q. Who was known as "Angel Of The Mining Camps?"

A. Nellie Cashman.

———— ?¿ ————

Q. What ubiquitous Arizona pioneer claimed to have raised the first U.S. flag over Tucson in 1856?

A. William Kirkland.

History

Q. What prisoners escaped from an east Phoenix compound Christmas Eve, 1944?

A. German prisoners of war.

———— ?¿ ————

Q. What was the name of the all-black Phoenix high school desegregated in the summer of 1953?

A. George Washington Carver High School.

———— ?¿ ————

Q. Who was the captain of Topographic Engineers who led an ill-equipped exploration of northern Arizona in 1851?

A. Lorenzo Sitgreaves.

———— ?¿ ————

Q. What famed Dodge City gunslinger did Marshall Wyatt Earp recruit in 1881 to help him keep Tombstone quiet?

A. Bat Masterson.

———— ?¿ ————

Q. Tucson-reared Ignacio Bonillas returned to Mexico and occupied what high post during World War I?

A. Mexican ambassador to the U.S.

———— ?¿ ————

Q. Prescott's nightlife used to be concentrated in what long block opposite Courthouse Square?

A. Whiskey Row.

———— ?¿ ————

Q. Kidnap victim June Robles, 6, survived how many days entombment in 1934 before captors revealed her whereabouts?

A. Nineteen.

History

Q. Who was the Mojave chief who went to Washington in 1865 to view the Union's victory celebration?

A. Irataba.

———— ?¿ ————

Q. How many people died when an arsonist torched Tucson's Pioneer Hotel just before Christmas, 1970?

A. 29.

———— ?¿ ————

Q. What bloodthirsty pioneer was named "colonel" by the First Territorial Legislature for forays against Apaches?

A. King S. Woolsey.

———— ?¿ ————

Q. The 1871 "Wickenburg Massacre" was an outgrowth of what kind of crime?

A. A stagecoach robbery.

———— ?¿ ————

Q. Who was the skillful chief of scouts for the U.S. Army in Arizona under General Crook?

A. Al Sieber.

———— ?¿ ————

Q. Tucson pioneers provoked the wrath of easterners with what 1871 action against Apaches?

A. Camp Grant Massacre.

———— ?¿ ————

Q. Who was the frontier soldier, rancher and historian who became an expert on Southwestern place names?

A. Will Croft Barnes.

Q. What was the formal name of the huge northern Arizona ranch called "the Hashknife outfit?"

A. Aztec Land and Cattle Company.

———— ?¿ ————

Q. What is the brand for the historic Babbitt Brothers cattle ranch in northern Arizona?

A. CO- (CO bar).

———— ?¿ ————

Q. Fort Whipple, established in 1864 to protect Arizona's first capital, has served what purpose since 1922?

A. A veterans' hospital.

———— ?¿ ————

Q. Territorial explorer Amiel W. Whipple, for whom Fort Whipple was named, died in what Civil War battle?

A. Chancellorsville.

———— ?¿ ————

Q. What early Fort Buchanan commander became a Confederate general despite the loss of one leg in battle?

A. Captain Richard S. Ewell.

———— ?¿ ————

Q. Who was removed from command of the Army Department of Arizona in 1871 for "soft" Indian policies?

A. General George Stoneman.

———— ?¿ ————

Q. What Bradshaw Mountain tunnel allowed mules to haul ore from mine to railhead?

A. Poland Tunnel.

History

Q. What was the name of Arizona's first narrow-gauge railroad, powered by mules in 1879, steam in 1880?

A. The Coronado Railroad.

———— ?¿ ————

Q. What famous Virginia & Truckee steam locomotive is displayed at Old Tucson?

A. *Reno.*

———— ?¿ ————

Q. What famous locomotive from Utah's 1869 Golden Spike ceremony became No. 1 on the Gila Valley, Globe & Northern?

A. *Jupiter.*

———— ?¿ ————

Q. What projected railroad from Globe to Flagstaff left only the adit of an aborted tunnel in the Mogollon Rim?

A. The Arizona Mineral Belt.

———— ?¿ ————

Q. Where was the first permanent U.S. military post established in Arizona in 1851?

A. Fort Defiance.

———— ?¿ ————

Q. What cursed impediments of Kearny's Army of the West may have been the first wheeled vehicles across Arizona?

A. Two cannon.

———— ?¿ ————

Q. Where was Arizona's first post office established in 1856?

A. Fort Defiance.

History

Q. Where was the first permanent U.S. military post in southern Arizona established in 1857?

A. Fort Buchanan.

———— ?¿ ————

Q. Southern Arizona was once part of what vast New Mexico county?

A. Dona Ana.

———— ?¿ ————

Q. What western Arizona fort, established in 1859, guarded wagon and steamboat supply routes to the interior?

A. Fort Mojave.

———— ?¿ ————

Q. What planned mining town, begun in 1953, shows evidence of Del Webb's later retirement town architecture?

A. San Manuel.

———— ?¿ ————

Q. Where is the only Indian-fighting post in Arizona still an active military installation?

A. Fort Huachuca.

———— ?¿ ————

Q. What town had its first jail cells blasted out of solid rock in a mountainside?

A. Clifton.

———— ?¿ ————

Q. The cruiser U.S.S. Phoenix was sold and later sunk during what war?

A. The Falkland Islands War, 1982.

Q. What kind of 400-mile, 27-station communication system predated the military telegraph in Arizona?

A. Heliograph (mirrors).

——— ?¿ ———

Q. Near the San Pedro River the Mormon Battalion fought a bloody battle with what kind of creatures?

A. Wild bulls.

Q. What year did a Tucson physician's steam Locomobile become the first recorded automobile in Arizona?

A. 1900.

Q. Who was the first president to visit Arizona?

A. William McKinley (1901).

Q. Hunt's Tomb in Papago Park contains the remains of George W.P. Hunt, his wife and how many of her kin?

A. Her parents and sister.

——— ?¿ ———

Q. What town claims to have built the nation's first municipal airport in 1919?

A. Tucson.

——— ?¿ ———

Q. What was the name given the child of Forty-niners, believed to be the first Anglo child born in Arizona?

A. Gila Howard.

Q. In what year was Arizona State College at Flagstaff renamed Northern Arizona University?

A. 1966.

———— ?¿ ————

Q. What frontier cavalry captain was later a general, and father of a U.S. Army general?

A. Adna R. Chaffee.

———— ?¿ ————

Q. What Arizona National Guard regiment became the honored "Bushmasters" of World War II?

A. 158th Infantry.

———— ?¿ ————

Q. Who was the Arizona helicopter pilot who received the Congressional Medal of Honor during the Tet offensive in Vietnam?

A. Warrant Officer Fred Ferguson.

———— ?¿ ————

Q. Who was the Marine sergeant from Globe who became a hero among U.S. hostages in Iran 1979-81?

A. Jimmy Lopez.

———— ?¿ ————

Q. What World War II hero lost both feet but kept fighting Germans and won the Congressional Medal?

A. Sylvestre Herrera.

———— ?¿ ————

Q. What pioneer explorer, called "The Mormon Pathfinder," is buried at Alpine?

A. Jacob Hamblin.

———— ?¿ ————

Q. Who was the Confederate captain whose small troop occupied Tucson in 1862?

A. Sherod Hunter.

——— ?¿ ———

Q. Why did U.S. senators from the South favor the Gadsden Purchase?

A. As a southern railroad route.

——— ?¿ ———

Q. What underworld figure, living in Phoenix as "William Nelson," was blown to bits Nov. 4, 1955?

A. Willie Biof.

——— ?¿ ———

Q. How many outlaws were executed or lynched for the "Bisbee Massacre" holdup in 1884?

A. Six.

——— ?¿ ———

Q. What leading promoter of Arizona Territory was jailed in 1862 for being a Confederate sympathizer?

A. Sylvester Mowry.

——— ?¿ ———

Q. Who were the World War I draft dodgers whose shootout with lawmen netted them 42 1/2 years in prison?

A. Tom and John Power.

——— ?¿ ———

Q. A flip invitation to what 1899 event brought the wrath of President McKinley down on Sheriff F.J. Wattron?

A. The hanging of murderer George Smiley.

——— ?¿ ———

Q. What high school was moved from downtown Phoenix in 1988 after 50 years in the same location?

A. St. Mary's.

History

Q. What famous gangster was arrested by Tucson police January 29, 1934?

A. John Dillinger.

———— ?ι ————

Q. What resourceful mountain man and guide is buried on the grounds of Sharlot Hall Museum, Prescott?

A. Pauline Weaver.

———— ?ι ————

Q. An 1872 military wagon road from Fort Apache to Camp Verde has been traced out and named what?

A. General Crook Trail.

———— ?ι ————

Q. The design of Arizona's state flag was controversial when legislators approved it in what year?

A. 1917.

———— ?ι ————

Q. Sun City opened January 1, 1960; when was its last lot sold?

A. 1978.

———— ?ι ————

Q. What famous frontiersman led an expedition against the Navajos of northern Arizona in 1863?

A. Kit Carson.

———— ?ι ————

Q. What Apache Junction marker became one of Arizona's first roadside monuments more than 50 years ago?

A. The Lost Dutchman monument.

———— ?ι ————

Q. Where did Arizona's first shopping center open in 1939?

A. Tucson.

———— ?ᵢ ————

Q. What famous aviator helped dedicate Tucson's second municipal airport in 1927?

A. Charles A. Lindbergh.

———— ?ᵢ ————

Q. Who was held captive by Indians for six years after the 1851 massacre of her family?

A. Olive Oatman.

———— ?ᵢ ————

Q. What famous mine was most responsible for Bisbee's long prosperity?

A. The Copper Queen.

———— ?ᵢ ————

Q. Who was the Montana senator whose United Verde properties caused Jerome's first boom?

A. William Andrews Clark.

———— ?ᵢ ————

Q. What was the cute name of the one-locomotive railroad opened in 1915 to serve a mine near Dos Cabezas?

A. Mascot & Western.

———— ?ᵢ ————

Q. When did the last steamboats ply the lower Colorado River?

A. 1916.

———— ?ᵢ ————

Q. What was the name of the gold mine that kept Oatman booming during the first four decades of this century?

A. The Tom Reed Mine.

———— ?¿ ————

Q. What leader hoped the Colorado River could supply his Deseret empire if it went to war with the United States?

A. Brigham Young.

———— ?¿ ————

Q. What was the occupation of Captain Jack Mellon?

A. Steamboat captain.

———— ?¿ ————

Q. What Mexican War contingent pioneered a National Wagon Road across Arizona in 1846?

A. The Mormon Battalion.

———— ?¿ ————

Q. Colonel Stephen Watts Kearny's "Army Of The West" followed what river en route to California?

A. The Gila.

———— ?¿ ————

Q. Outlaw traffic caused the canyon of what river to be called "The Back Door To Arizona"?

A. Blue River.

———— ?¿ ————

Q. What gunman survived the O.K. Corral fight in 1881 but was later killed by an Apache County deputy sheriff?

A. Ike Clanton.

———— ?¿ ————

Q. Who was the Apache County Sheriff who gunned down three men and a boy in less than a minute in 1887?

A. Commodore Perry Owens.

Q. Who was the real-life rancher and sheriff on whose life the TV series "Sheriff of Cochise" was based?

A. John H. Slaughter.

——— ?¿ ———

Q. What military post, begun in 1868 to protect the road through Apache Pass, is now a national historic site?

A. Fort Bowie.

——— ?¿ ———

Q. What year was Fort Apache deactivated?

A. 1924.

——— ?¿ ———

Q. Overflow from Roosevelt Dam was captured April 14, 1915, to christen what vessel?

A. The battleship *U.S.S. Arizona*.

——— ?¿ ———

Q. A telephone company building in downtown Phoenix was the first to use refrigerated air conditioning in what year?

A. 1928.

——— ?¿ ———

Q. Who was the black man who entered Arizona with the first European explorers?

A. Estevancio.

——— ?¿ ———

Q. In what year was the U.S. Border Patrol formed?

A. 1924.

——— ?¿ ———

Q. A cave on Salt River where soldiers massacred dozens of Yavapai Indians in 1872 is called what?

History

A. Skull Cave.

———— ?¿ ————

Q. Who was the peripatetic frontiersman who fancied the title "Father of Arizona?"

A. Charles D. Poston.

———— ?¿ ————

Q. What race of infantrymen and cavalrymen were called "Buffalo Soldiers" because of their short, curly hair?

A. Blacks.

———— ?¿ ————

Q. What well-known couple ran the ferry at Parker before the Colorado River was bridged in 1937?

A. Joe and Nellie Bush.

———— ?¿ ————

Q. King Carlos V of Spain replaced Jesuits in the New World with missionaries from which order?

A. Franciscans.

———— ?¿ ————

Q. Where are the oldest ruins of Spanish structures in Arizona, dating to 1628?

A. The Hopi Reservation.

———— ?¿ ————

Q. What Hopi village was wiped out by fellow tribesmen in 1700 because the village embraced Catholicism?

A. Awatovi.

———— ?¿ ————

Q. Don Lorenzo Hubbell, best-known of Arizona's Indian traders, also was sheriff of what county?

A. Apache.

History

Q. What historic Ganado trading post is now protected by the National Park Service but still an active store?

A. Hubbell Trading Post National Historic Site.

——— ?¿ ———

Q. What member of the British royal family visited Arizona with her entourage in 1965?

A. Princess Margaret.

——— ?¿ ———

Q. What air force installation began as Tucson's municipal airport in 1927?

A. Davis-Monthan Air Force Base.

——— ?¿ ———

Q. What venerable school closed in 1990 after nearly a century of operation?

A. Phoenix Indian School.

——— ?¿ ———

Q. The accidental burning of a seaplane on Roosevelt Lake in 1927 caused tension between the U.S. and what nation?

A. Italy.

——— ?¿ ———

Q. In Arizona's first airshow in 1910, an airplane won a race with what kind of conveyance?

A. A Studebaker automobile.

——— ?¿ ———

Q. What did Lucius Copeland of Phoenix invent in the 1890s, about the time gasoline engines were invented?

A. A steam motorcycle.

History

Q. What New Mexico village could technically be called Arizona's first "county seat?"

A. Mesilla.

———— ?ι ————

Q. Who was the mountain man whose 1825-26 travels provided the first English description of Arizona?

A. James Ohio Pattie.

———— ?ι ————

Q. What Phoenix newspaper, largest in Arizona, celebrated its centennial in 1990?

A. *The Arizona Republic.*

———— ?ι ————

Q. What legendary transportation system ran through Arizona until the Civil War forced it northward?

A. The Butterfield Stage Line.

———— ?ι ————

Q. What happened to the original community of San Carlos?

A. It is now under the waters of San Carlos Lake.

———— ?ι ————

Q. What New York City mayor spent his boyhood as son of an Army bandmaster at Forts Huachuca and Whipple?

A. Fiorello A. LaGuardia.

———— ?ι ————

Q. What western showman sunk much of his fortune into a mine on the north slope of the Santa Catalina Mountains?

A. Colonel William F. "Buffalo Bill" Cody.

Q. Who was the arms manufacturer who took control of the historic Patagonia Mine?

A. Samuel F. Colt.

——— ?₂ ———

Q. What statehood proposal did Arizona voters reject in 1906?

A. Joint statehood with New Mexico.

——— ?₂ ———

Q. The western hemisphere's first bombing raid was in 1913 by a homemade airplane taking off from where?

A. Douglas.

——— ?₂ ———

Q. Who was the first black West Point graduate, later a political figure in Nogales, Arizona?

A. Henry O. Flipper.

——— ?₂ ———

Q. What vintage is the steamboat Charles H. Spencer, submerged in the Colorado River at Lees Ferry?

A. 1911.

——— ?₂ ———

Q. Who was Arizona's hapless female stagecoach robber?

A. Pearl Hart.

——— ?₂ ———

Q. What other shady Pearl lived her last years in Douglas and is buried there?

A. Pearl Starr, daughter of Belle Starr.

History

Q. What Arizona town has preserved its "jail tree," to which prisoners were chained in the 19th century?

A. Wickenburg.

——— ?¿ ———

Q. What legendary Tombstone figure spent much of the last years of his life as a "desert rat" near Parker?

A. Wyatt Earp.

——— ?¿ ———

Q. Who was the Phoenix-area farmer whose friends called him "The Broccoli King of America" in the 1940s?

A. John M. Jacobs.

——— ?¿ ———

Q. How many brothers were involved in the Babbitt Brothers trading and ranching empire in northern Arizona?

A. Five.

——— ?¿ ———

Q. What state park preserves the side-by-side mansions of two brothers who pioneered Arizona's lumbering industry?

A. Riordan State Park, Flagstaff.

——— ?¿ ———

Q. What monument on the U.S.-Mexico border celebrates the entry of a Spanish explorer into Arizona?

A. Coronado National Memorial.

——— ?¿ ———

Q. What was the name of the robust camp follower and early Yuma resident known as "The Great Western?"

A. Sarah Bowman.

History

Q. What 1930s Phoenix trunk murderess did the press label "Tiger Woman?"

A. Winnie Ruth Judd.

———— ?¿ ————

Q. The Winnie Ruth Judd murder case involved two victims, Hedvig Samuelson and Agnes Anne LeRoi. Whom was Judd convicted of killing?

A. LeRoi.

———— ?¿ ————

Q. What early Phoenix developer, farmer and booster is said to have introduced palm trees from Egypt?

A. Dwight B. Heard.

———— ?¿ ————

Q. What was the occupation of "Old Bill" Williams, who gave his name to several Arizona features?

A. Mountain man.

———— ?¿ ————

Q. Who was the Taos trapper, trader and guide who led several U.S. government expeditions across Arizona?

A. Antoine Leroux.

———— ?¿ ————

Q. Which U.S. president signed the act making Arizona a separate territory?

A. Abraham Lincoln.

———— ?¿ ————

Q. What was the name of the last major battle between hostile Apaches and whites in Arizona July 17, 1882?

A. The Battle of Big Dry Wash.

History

Q. There is no Big Dry Wash on Arizona maps. Where was the Battle of Big Dry Wash fought?

A. East Clear Creek.

——— ?¿ ———

Q. What is the name of the restored Victorian dwelling built in 1895 by an early Phoenix physician?

A. Rosson House.

——— ?¿ ———

Q. What's the name of the historic ford used by Spain, Mexico and the United States to reach California?

A. Yuma Crossing.

——— ?¿ ———

Q. Juan Bautista de Anza led an expedition from Tubac in 1775 that founded what city?

A. San Francisco.

——— ?¿ ———

Q. What one-armed explorer led the first river expedition through the Grand Canyon in 1869?

A. Major John Wesley Powell.

——— ?¿ ———

Q. A Pima County legislator was booed and pelted with vegetables when he brought home what patronage prize?

A. The University of Arizona.

——— ?¿ ———

Q. What did newspapers call the territorial legislature that divided up institutions on the basis of patronage?

A. "The Thieving Thirteenth."

Q. Where was Arizona Territory's first newspaper, *The Weekly Arizonian*, published in 1859?

A. Tubac.

———— ?¿ ————

Q. What central Arizona town got its name from its role as a key Indian fighting post in the 1870s and '80s?

A. Camp Verde.

———— ?¿ ————

Q. What was the name of the malaria-ridden outpost that preceded Camp Verde?

A. Camp Lincoln.

———— ?¿ ————

Q. What year did Arizona begin paving the old Black Canyon stagecoach road, now part of Interstate 17?

A. 1946.

———— ?¿ ————

Q. Who was the "Baron of Arizona" whose fraudulent Spanish land grant claimed 11 million acres?

A. James Addison Reavis.

———— ?¿ ————

Q. What tire company owned vast Arizona cotton farms to provide cords for their product?

A. Goodyear Tire & Rubber Co.

———— ?¿ ————

Q. Who gave his name to a landmark U.S. Supreme Court decision, then died in a downtown Phoenix knife fight?

A. Ernesto Miranda.

Q. Who was Arizona's top-ranked visitor in 1987?

A. Pope John Paul II.

———— ?¿ ————

Q. Where was Arizona's infamous Territorial Prison located?

A. Yuma.

———— ?¿ ————

Q. What Gila River town replaced Yuma in 1909 as site of the territorial (later state) prison?

A. Florence.

———— ?¿ ————

Q. The false clock on the 1891 Pinal County Courthouse in Florence always stands at what hour?

A. 11:45.

———— ?¿ ————

Q. What year did Navajo Bridge replace Lees Ferry?

A. 1929.

———— ?¿ ————

Q. What trail was named because Arizona LDS pioneers preferred to be married in the St. George Temple?

A. "The Honeymoon Trail."

———— ?¿ ————

Q. What year did the Santa Fe, Prescott & Phoenix Railroad connect Phoenix to the Santa Fe mainline?

A. 1895.

———— ?¿ ————

Q. The Phoenix street railway begun in the 1880s later served what rural town?

A. Glendale.

——— ?¿ ———

Q. Who was the Bisbee prospector whose photo was a model for the miner on Arizona's state seal?

A. George Warren.

——— ?¿ ———

Q. Where was the Yavapai County dam that broke in 1890, killing more than 60 people?

A. Walnut Grove.

——— ?¿ ———

Q. What pioneer developer built Grand Avenue to promote farming northwest of Phoenix?

A. W.J. Murphy.

——— ?¿ ———

Q. For what crime was Jack Swilling wrongly imprisoned at the end of his life?

A. Stagecoach robbery.

——— ?¿ ———

Q. Who was the murderer whose decapitation in 1930 caused Arizona to forego hanging in capital crimes?

A. Eva Dugan.

——— ?¿ ———

Q. An early Salt River Valley industry was built on the plumes of what awkward fowl?

A. The ostrich.

——— ?¿ ———

Q. Where did two airliners crash in 1956 in the worst commercial aviation disaster to that date?

A. The Grand Canyon.

History

Q. What year were the Arizona Rangers established to fight rampant cattle rustling?
A. 1901.

———— ?¿ ————

Q. Northern Arizona University was originally built as what kind of institution?
A. A reform school.

———— ?¿ ————

Q. What famed general was sent to Arizona twice to quell the "Indian problem"?
A. General George C. Crook.

———— ?¿ ————

Q. What sort of vehicle was the General Jesup?
A. A Colorado River steamboat.

———— ?¿ ————

Q. Who was General Crook's aide whose writings about frontier Arizona are still popular?
A. John G. Bourke.

———— ?¿ ————

Q. What is Arizona's oldest institution of higher learning, established in 1885 as a normal school?
A. Arizona State University.

———— ?¿ ————

Q. What officer accepted the final surrender of Geronimo in 1886?
A. General Nelson A. Miles.

———— ?¿ ————

Q. What Mormon Battalion officer tried to navigate the Gila River in a makeshift flatboat?

A. Lieutenant George Stoneman.

———— ?¿ ————

Q. In what year did Phoenix get its first paved streets?

A. 1911.

———— ?¿ ————

Q. When was the first ice manufacturing plant established in Phoenix?

A. 1879.

———— ?¿ ————

Q. In what decade did factory-built evaporative coolers become available?

A. The 1930s.

NATIVE AMERICANS

CHAPTER FOUR

Q. What is the name of the largest Indian tribe, headquartered in Arizona?

A. Navajo.

———?¿———

Q. What remarkable woman preserved her heritage in two books, *A Pima Remembers* and *Pima Indian Legends*?

A. Anna Moore Shaw.

———?¿———

Q. What do Hopis call the figures of their deities?

A. Kachinas.

———?¿———

Q. How many Indian reservations are there in Arizona?

A. 22.

———?¿———

Q. A heroic statue at Central Avenue and Thomas Road in Phoenix celebrates what famous World War II group?

A. Navajo "Code Talkers."

Native Americans

Q. What group of Mexican Indians occupies several enclaves in Arizona?

A. Yaquis.

———— ?¿ ————

Q. Pima Indian Ira Hayes became a World War II hero by participating in what feat?

A. Raising the U.S. flag on Iwo Jima.

———— ?¿ ————

Q. Who is the Navajo painter who is the only artist represented in New York's Metropolitan Museum?

A. R.C. Gorman.

———— ?¿ ————

Q. What people are noted for their multicolored corn?

A. Hopi.

———— ?¿ ————

Q. What is the name of the paper-thin Hopi bread made with blue corn meal?

A. Piki.

———— ?¿ ————

Q. What kind of plant fibers do Papago women use to weave their popular baskets?

A. Yucca.

———— ?¿ ————

Q. What hereditary White Mountain Apache chief won a Congressional Medal of Honor and visited Washington, D.C.?

A. Alchesay.

Native Americans

Q. What is the native name of the Indian tribe known historically to white men as "Yumas?"

A. Quechan.

———————?¿———————

Q. What small tribe of Colorado River Indians number about 800, half of whom live in Mexico?

A. Cocopah.

———————?¿———————

Q. On what string of communities did early Anglo travelers depend for supplies?

A. The Pima Villages.

———————?¿———————

Q. What Arizona Indian reservation is entirely surrounded by the lands of the tribe's historic opponents?

A. The Hopi Reservation.

———————?¿———————

Q. The Papago people, so named by Spaniards, have readopted what ancient name in their own language?

A. Tohono O'odham.

———————?¿———————

Q. What populous Arizona groups call themselves a nation?

A. The Navajo Nation.

———————?¿———————

Q. What venerated Navajo leader was daughter of the last traditional "chief," Henry Chee Dodge?

A. Annie Wauneka.

Native Americans

Q. When were Native Americans first permitted to vote in Arizona?

A. 1948.

———— ?¿ ————

Q. With what group have the Hopis been engaged in a territorial dispute for generations?

A. Navajos.

———— ?¿ ————

Q. When was the first portion of the huge Navajo Reservation set aside?

A. 1868.

———— ?¿ ————

Q. The Navajo Reservation is said to be larger than what eastern state?

A. West Virginia.

———— ?¿ ————

Q. How many Apache army scouts won the Congressional Medal of Honor?

A. Ten.

———— ?¿ ————

Q. What prisoner of war rode in President Theodore Roosevelt's inaugural parade in 1905?

A. Geronimo.

———— ?¿ ————

Q. What is the range of present estimates of the Navajo Reservation's population?

A. 150,000 to 200,000.

Native Americans

Q. A short-lived executive order by which president included Phoenix and Tempe in the Salt River Indian Reservation?

A. Rutherford B. Hayes (1879).

―――――?¿―――――

Q. Where are Hualapai tribal headquarters?

A. Peach Springs.

―――――?¿―――――

Q. What kind of "painting" yields Navajo religious drawings?

A. Sandpainting.

―――――?¿―――――

Q. Tradition says Cochise was buried at Cochise Stronghold in what mountain range?

A. Dragoon.

―――――?¿―――――

Q. Native Americans have begun demanding that what be returned from eastern museums?

A. The bones of their ancestors.

―――――?¿―――――

Q. What do pueblo people call their ceremonial chambers?

A. Kivas.

―――――?¿―――――

Q. What large ruin near Whiteriver was apparently a cosmopolitan community in prehistoric times?

A. Kinishba.

Native Americans

Q. What Verde Valley national monument preserves ruins of an important trade center where prehistoric Hohokam and Sinagua mingled?

A. Tuzigoot.

———— ?¿ ————

Q. What Zuni city, now a ruin, was the destination of Coronado's expedition in 1540?

A. Hawikuh.

———— ?¿ ————

Q. What did Hopis fear that the "monster" represented by Spaniards and their horses would do to them?

A. Eat them.

———— ?¿ ————

Q. What do Navajos call their forced march to Bosque Redondo, N.M., in 1864-65?

A. The Long Walk.

———— ?¿ ————

Q. What government body has established a park in Monument Valley?

A. The Navajo Nation.

———— ?¿ ————

Q. A hump-backed musician, adapted by modern Indians from Anasazi petroglyphs, plays what instrument?

A. Flute.

———— ?¿ ————

Q. Descendants of Apache scouts have an unwritten agreement that lets them gather what from Fort Huachuca?

A. Acorns.

Native Americans

Q. Darvin Burnette, the last surviving Apache scout for the Army, died in what year?

A. 1988.

————?¿————

Q. The Army's employment of Apache scouts, begun in 1871, ended in what year?

A. 1947.

————?¿————

Q. What is the capital of the White Mountain Apache Reservation?

A. Whiteriver.

————?¿————

Q. What is the capital of the Tohono O'odham (Papago) nation?

A. Sells.

————?¿————

Q. About how many Paiutes are on the rolls of the Kaibab Reservation headquartered at Moccasin?

A. 220.

————?¿————

Q. What desert people ritually use long poles to harvest the fruit of the saguaro?

A. Tohono O'odham (Papago).

————?¿————

Q. Hohokam people occupied the place archaeologists call Snaketown for how long?

A. 1,400 years.

Native Americans

Q. Of what tribe was Ida Redbird, who brought about a rejuvenation of her people's pottery-making in the 1930s?

A. Maricopa.

———— ?¿ ————

Q. Two Grey Hills is a place name and also denotes a premium quality in what product?

A. Navajo rugs.

———— ?¿ ————

Q. Where are the ruins of a Spanish church that date back to 1629?

A. Awatovi on the Hopi Reservation.

———— ?¿ ————

Q. What is the name of the large Pima Indian reservation along Interstate 10 south of Phoenix?

A. Gila River Reservation.

———— ?¿ ————

Q. What do Navajos call the figures of their spirits?

A. Yeibichai.

———— ?¿ ————

Q. The ruins at Montezuma Castle and Montezuma Well were built by what prehistoric culture?

A. Sinagua.

———— ?¿ ————

Q. What's the literal meaning of Sinagua, name of a prehistoric Arizona culture?

A. Without water.

Native Americans

Q. Cliff paintings in Canyon de Chelly depict the travels of early intruders from what country?

A. Spain.

———?¿———

Q. What Athapascan peoples apparently arrived in the Southwest not long before the Spaniards?

A. Navajos and Apaches.

———?¿———

Q. How is Canyon de Chelly's Standing Cow Ruin identified?

A. By Navajo pictograph.

———?¿———

Q. What native uprising in 1751 prompted Spain to establish the Presidio of Tubac?

A. Pima Rebellion.

———?¿———

Q. What 1680 rebellion forced Spanish missionaries to leave the Hopi villages?

A. The Pueblo Revolt.

———?¿———

Q. What northern Arizona people thwarted all efforts of Catholic missionaries to convert them?

A. Hopis.

———?¿———

Q. The present religion of what Indian group blends Catholic ceremony with its own native beliefs?

A. Tohono O'odham.

Native Americans

Q. The social dance music of today's Piman peoples goes by what name?

A. Chicken scratch.

——— ?¿ ———

Q. The traditional six or eight-sided Navajo dwelling is called what?

A. Hogan.

——— ?¿ ———

Q. Who was the first female tribal leader of the Hualapai people?

A. Carrie Bender.

——— ?¿ ———

Q. The Sunrise Dance is one of several in what four-day Apache ceremony?

A. Puberty rites for maidens.

——— ?¿ ———

Q. What do Navajos call themselves?

A. *Dineh*, "The People."

——— ?¿ ———

Q. What is the name of the political subdivision from which a Navajo tribal councilman is elected?

A. Chapter.

——— ?¿ ———

Q. Whose rare collection of Hopi kachina dolls is now housed in the Heard Museum?

A. Former U.S. Senator Barry Goldwater's.

Native Americans

Q. Phoenix Indian School's football team was daunting in its day, but what other school "team" was more famous?

A. The Phoenix Indian School Marching Band.

————?¿————

Q. What is the name of the sacred peak southwest of Tucson where Papago (Tohono O'odham) dieties dwell?

A. Baboquivari.

————?¿————

Q. Who became Arizona's first Native American legislator in 1967?

A. Lloyd House.

————?¿————

Q. The best-known silverwork of one group of Native American silversmiths is called Hopi _____.

A. Overlay.

————?¿————

Q. What tribe's silverwork is characterized by heavy, graceful shapes of silver cast in sand?

A. Navajo.

————?¿————

Q. Chief Cochise and renegade leader Geronimo belonged to what Apache group?

A. Chiricahua.

————?¿————

Q. What is the only type of basket traditionally woven by Navajos?

A. The wedding basket.

Native Americans

Q. What is the best-known religious ceremony of the Yaqui people?

A. The Deer Dance.

———— ?¿ ————

Q. What Hopi prayer for rain, now cloistered, has always intrigued outsiders for less than religious reasons?

A. The snake dance.

———— ?¿ ————

Q. What northern Arizona peaks are sacred to both Navajos and Hopis?

A. San Francisco Peaks.

———— ?¿ ————

Q. When was Arizona's newest Indian reservation, that of the Payson Tonto Apache band, set aside?

A. 1972.

———— ?¿ ————

Q. The White Mountain Apaches are one major group of Apaches today; what's the other group?

A. San Carlos.

———— ?¿ ————

Q. What central Arizona tribe was frequently confused with Apaches by early white settlers and soldiers?

A. Yavapais.

———— ?¿ ————

Q. What is the ethnic origin of many people in the Tempe suburb of Guadalupe?

A. Yaqui.

Native Americans

Q. Most of the ruins in Canyons de Chelly and del Muerto were built by members of what vanished culture?

A. The Anasazi.

———?¿———

Q. What modern "fiber" crop was grown by prehistoric Arizonans and traded among members of various cultures?

A. Cotton.

———?¿———

Q. What arch gives the name to the Navajo Nation's capital?

A. Window Rock.

———?¿———

Q. What is the former Anglo name for Kykotsmovi, capital of the Hopi tribe?

A. New Oraibi.

———?¿———

Q. What cliff dwelling was misnamed for an Aztec emperor?

A. Montezuma Castle.

———?¿———

Q. Members of what culture created the ruins at Tonto National Monument?

A. Salado.

———?¿———

Q. What complex of ruins north of Flagstaff showed traces of several prehistoric cultures, but mainly Sinagua?

A. Wupatki National Monument.

Native Americans

Q. Which is the oldest of the Hopi villages?

A. Walpi.

———— ?¿ ————

Q. Most Hopi villages are clustered on how many mesas?

A. Three.

———— ?¿ ————

Q. Hano on First Mesa was occupied by "mercenaries," defenders who fled from what New Mexico pueblo?

A. Tewa.

———— ?¿ ————

Q. Where is Navajo Community College located?

A. Tsaile.

———— ?¿ ————

Q. What 204-member group won federal recognition in 1990 as the nation's 509th Indian tribe?

A. San Juan Paiutes.

NAME GAMES

Q. What southern Arizona town was named for a sailing ship?

A. Oracle.

—————?¿—————

Q. What city was named during a celebration of the American Centennial July 4, 1876?

A. Flagstaff.

—————?¿—————

Q. What town was named by the outcome of a card game to decide ownership of a ranch?

A. Show Low.

—————?¿—————

Q. What name for a certain kind of mounted soldier was applied to a mountain range and community in Cochise County?

A. Dragoon.

—————?¿—————

Q. What former smelter town was named for France's World War I war minister?

A. Clemenceau.

Name Games

Q. What was the original name of the Phoenix suburb of Tempe?

A. Hayden's Ferry.

———— ?¿ ————

Q. What Arizona city name translates as "walnut?"

A. Nogales.

———— ?¿ ————

Q. "Ambos Nogales" means "both Nogales;" where is the second one?

A. Sonora, Mexico

———— ?¿ ————

Q. For what Spanish colonial military governor was the Mogollon Rim probably named?

A. Juan Ignacio Flores Mogollon, circa 1715.

———— ?¿ ————

Q. What was an earlier name for Morristown?

A. Hot Springs Junction.

———— ?¿ ————

Q. What northern Arizona landmark is named for an extraterrestrial visitor?

A. Meteor Crater.

———— ?¿ ————

Q. Early explorers and railroad builders had a devil of a time crossing what canyon east of Flagstaff?

A. Canyon Diablo.

———— ?¿ ————

Q. What is the common name for the corner of Arizona north and west of the Colorado River?

Name Games

A. The Arizona Strip.

————?¿————

Q. What was Bullhead City named for?

A. A rock shaped like the head of a bull.

————?¿————

Q. What was the name of Hoover Dam when it was dedicated in 1936?

A. Boulder Dam.

————?¿————

Q. What post office name resulted from Arizona's most famous clerical goof?

A. "Cornville" for "Coaneville."

————?¿————

Q. Grammatically, what's wrong with the name Picacho Peak?

A. It's redundant. Picacho means "peak" in Spanish.

————?¿————

Q. Early explorers called one river " Bill Williams Fork." What is its modern name?

A. The Big Sandy.

————?¿————

Q. Darrel Dupa named Tempe for what classic place?

A. The Vale of Tempe in Greece.

————?¿————

Q. Tombstone newspapers included the *Nugget* and the *Prospector,* but what was the most apt name of all?

A. *The Epitaph.*

Name Games

Q. What landmark is named for a child's play fort that provided cover during a real 1866 Indian attack?

A. Fort Rock.

———— ?¿ ————

Q. For what was Superior named?

A. Arizona and Lake Superior Mining Co.

———— ?¿ ————

Q. "Mogollon" probably originated with a Spanish governor, but it may have come from what other Spanish term?

A. The word for "parasite" or "hanger-on."

———— ?¿ ————

Q. For what was modest Mammoth named?

A. The Mammoth Mine, ca. 1872.

———— ?¿ ————

Q. What community name do some Punkin Center residents prefer?

A. Tonto Basin.

———— ?¿ ————

Q. For whom was Prescott named?

A. Historian William Hickling Prescott.

———— ?¿ ————

Q. What national monument protects an ancient Hohokam ruin whose Spanish name translates as "Big House?"

A. Casa Grande.

———— ?¿ ————

Q. A postmark from what northern Arizona hamlet is valued in February?

Name Games

A. Valentine.

———¿———

Q. What hamlet is named for a melancholy color?

A. Blue.

———¿———

Q. The name of what Arizona river means "red" in Spanish?

A. Colorado.

———¿———

Q. The name of what Arizona river means "green" in Spanish?

A. Verde.

———¿———

Q. What town was named for the cousin of Winston Churchill's mother?

A. Jerome.

———¿———

Q. What early Spanish name for Arizona related to the native inhabitants?

A. Pimeria Alta, "land of the upper Pima."

———¿———

Q. What boulevard was named by horseback show-offs in the days when it ran along Tucson's northern edge?

A. Speedway.

———¿———

Q. What was the name of the Globe neighborhood where Governor Rose Mofford spent her childhood?

A. Six-shooter Canyon.

113

Name Games

Q. What unexpected Arizona town is named for a Nebraska town?

A. Surprise.

———— *?ₜ* ————

Q. What historic roadside hamlet matches the name of a John Steinbeck novel?

A. Tortilla Flat.

———— *?ₜ* ————

Q. The name of what town means "garlic" in Spanish?

A. Ajo.

———— *?ₜ* ————

Q. What was the original name of Lake Pleasant north of Sun City?

A. Frog Tanks.

———— *?ₜ* ————

Q. What was the political-sounding name of a rich gold-mining camp northwest of Phoenix?

A. Congress.

———— *?ₜ* ————

Q. What well-known mine in the Bradshaw Mountains might have been a companion to Congress?

A. Senator.

———— *?ₜ* ————

Q. What tree lent its name to nine Arizona canyons, six creeks, seven springs, a basin and various other landforms?

A. Sycamore.

Name Games

Q. Yavapai County maps showed Taul Creek until 1968 when experts realized "Taul" was 1900 cowboy talk for what?

A. Towel.

———?¿———

Q. The name Nutrioso is a compound of Spanish words for what animal?

A. Beaver and bear.

———?¿———

Q. What was the original name of Mesa?

A. Zenos.

———?¿———

Q. What city calls its mainstreet Deuce of Clubs Avenue?

A. Show Low.

———?¿———

Q. "Alamo" is a common name in Arizona. What does the Spanish word mean?

A. Cottonwood.

———?¿———

Q. Major John Wesly Powell said he named Bright Angel Creek because it contrasted so with what Utah river?

A. The Dirty Devil.

———?¿———

Q. A gaping open pit mine in the heart of Bisbee got its pastel name from what former mine superintendent?

A. Lavendar Pit, for Harrison Morrison Lavendar.

Name Games

Q. What is the true name of the mountain range frequently called "the Grahams"?

A. Pinaleno Mountains.

———— ?¿ ————

Q. What's another name for "A" Mountain, the Tucson peak which carries the University of Arizona initial?

A. Sentinel Peak.

———— ?¿ ————

Q. What is the name of the place where Brigham Young's son John established Fort Moroni in 1881?

A. Fort Valley.

———— ?¿ ————

Q. Name a festive-sounding copper mining camp south of Globe that no longer exists.

A. Christmas.

———— ?¿ ————

Q. What northern Arizona community was named for a Wyoming stagecoach robber?

A. Happy Jack.

———— ?¿ ————

Q. What Navajo County city was named by combining the surnames of two Mormon pioneers?

A. Snowflake.

———— ?¿ ————

Q. Anglo pronunciation of a Hopi leader's name was instrumental in giving what community its unusual name?

A. Tuba City.

Name Games

Q. What vanished Yavapai County mining camp was given a musical name by its eight owners?

A. Octave.

———————?¿———————

Q. Two large rocks gave shelter to Mormon pioneers in what Arizona Strip valley?

A. House Rock.

———————?¿———————

Q. What 4,100-foot peak in the Tucson Mountains was named in 1988 for a famous fighting unit?

A. Bushmaster Peak.

———————?¿———————

Q. What mountain man lent his name to mountains and a mining district in southern Yavapai County?

A. Pauline Weaver.

———————?¿———————

Q. The desperate attempt by cornered Apaches to escape soldiers' guns is remembered in the name of what landmark?

A. Apache Leap.

———————?¿———————

Q. What is the heady name of one formerly raucous neighborhood in Bisbee?

A. Brewery Gulch.

———————?¿———————

Q. After a notorious raid in 1953, the polygamist colony called Short Creek was renamed what?

A. Colorado City.

Name Games

Q. What was the apt name of the route where hundreds of immigrants died en route to California gold fields?

A. Camino del Diablo.

———— ?¿ ————

Q. What was the name of the White Mountain hostelry run by a former Army scout married to two Apache sisters?

A. Cooley ranch, for Corydon E. Cooley.

———— ?¿ ————

Q. Who was Scottsdale's founder, a chaplain whose name sounded like that of a famous general?

A. Major Winfield Scott.

———— ?¿ ————

Q. What's the name of the southeastern Arizona Canyon where Geronimo finally surrendered?

A. Skeleton Canyon.

———— ?¿ ————

Q. The place now known as San Carlos had another name before 1930. What was it?

A. Rice.

Q. What pass southwest of Winslow was named for the officer who escorted the first governor in Arizona?

A. Chavez Pass.

———— ?¿ ————

Q. What former U.S. president reluctantly showed up in 1930 to help dedicate a dam named for him?

A. Calvin Coolidge.

Name Games

Q. Bill, a Flagstaff hardware merchant, and brother Walter, founder of a women's wear chain, pronounced their surname differently. What was it?

A. Switzer.

—————?¿—————

Q. Ebenezer Bryce, for whom Utah's Bryce Canyon was named, is buried at what Arizona hamlet?

A. Bryce.

—————?¿—————

Q. Scout Dan O'Leary, for whom a peak is named, saved General George Crook from a massacre at what post in1872?

A. Camp Date Creek.

—————?¿—————

Q. What border hamlet was named for the ancestral home of the Scots who owned the San Rafael land grant?

A. Lochiel.

—————?¿—————

Q. For which prominent copper mining family is a southeastern Arizona border town named?

A. Douglas.

—————?¿—————

Q. Leroux Wash, Leroux Springs and Flagstaff's Leroux Street are named for whom?

A. Mountain man Antoine Leroux.

—————?¿—————

Q. For whom is the Phoenix district Maryvale named?

A. Mary Long, wife of developer John F. Long.

Name Games

Q. What lake near Flagstaff was named for the daughter of lumberman Timothy A. Riordan?

A. Lake Mary.

———— ?¿ ————

Q. What early Maricopa County town was named for a prophet from *The Book of Mormon*?

A. Lehi.

———— ?¿ ————

Q. How did Broadway Road in Phoenix get its name?

A. It was named for farmer Noah Broadway.

———— ?¿ ————

Q. In what community is Why Worry Lane?

A. Carefree.

———— ?¿ ————

Q. What did Emma Lee call her farm near Lees Ferry?

A. Lonely Dell.

———— ?¿ ————

Q. P.S. Knoll and P.S. Wildlife Area in the White Mountains are named for what pioneer rancher?

A. Pete Slaughter.

———— ?¿ ————

Q. When surveyors found they had incorrectly identified a mountain as Rincon Peak, what did they name it?

A. Wrong Mountain.

———— ?¿ ————

Q. What was the name of the Phoenix skid row and redlight district displaced in 1970 by Civic Plaza?

A. The Deuce.

ARTS & ENTERTAINMENT

Q. What movie director used Monument Valley as the location for "Stagecoach" in 1939?

A. John Ford.

———————?¿———————

Q. Old Tucson amusement park and movie location was established to film what 1940 movie?

A. "Arizona."

———————?¿———————

Q. What male actor's first starring role was opposite Jean Arthur in "Arizona?"

A. William Holden.

———————?¿———————

Q. The movie "Arizona" was based on a Saturday Evening Post serial written by what part-time Arizona resident?

A. Clarence Buddington Kelland.

———————?¿———————

Q. What radical, modern environmental author died in Tucson in 1989?

A. Edward Abbey.

121

Arts and Entertainment

Q. What Hollywood couple got married in Kingman March 30, 1939?

A. Clark Gable and Carole Lombard.

——— ?¿ ———

Q. What character actor was a native of Kingman?

A. Andy Devine.

——— ?¿ ———

Q. What villainous character actor graduated from Phoenix Union High School in 1937?

A. Jack Elam.

——— ?¿ ———

Q. What famous Arizona publication began in April, 1925, as a journal for engineers and road contractors?

A. *Arizona Highways.*

——— ?¿ ———

Q. What contemporary movie director grew up in Scottsdale?

A. Steven Spielberg.

——— ?¿ ———

Q. What western singer does Willcox honor with a yearly "day" in his honor?

A. Rex Allen.

——— ?¿ ———

Q. Name another singer who called Willcox home.

A. Tanya Tucker.

——— ?¿ ———

Q. Who is the singer whose 1987 album "Canciones De Mi Padre" celebrated her family's Tucson roots?

Arts and Entertainment

A. Linda Ronstadt.

————?⅋————

Q. What country singer began life dirt-poor in the town of Glendale, Arizona?

A. Marty Robbins.

————?⅋————

Q. What cowboy movie star was killed in an auto accident southeast of Florence October 12, 1940?

A. Tom Mix.

————?⅋————

Q. After his father was killed in an 1882 Indian attack, who became a well-known "Wild West" showman?

A. Arizona Charlie Meadows.

————?⅋————

Q. What 7,169-seat theater is billed as the largest single level theater in the nation?

A. Sundome (Sun City West).

————?⅋————

Q. Cudia City studios in Phoenix folded after what TV series died?

A. "Twenty-six Men."

————?⅋————

Q. Rex Allen proved unconvincing as the star of what short-lived TV series?

A. "Frontier Doctor."

————?⅋————

Q. What is the name of the Prescott businessmen's organization that annually presents "Indian" dances?

A. Smoki People.

Arts and Entertainment

Q. What was the original name of Phoenix' theater in-the-round, Celebrity Theater?

A. Phoenix Star Theater.

———— ?¿ ————

Q. What formerly world-renowned gossip spent his last years in obscurity in Scottsdale?

A. Walter Winchell.

———— ?¿ ————

Q. Who was the Wickenburg artisan credited with inventing the bola tie?

A. Vic Cedarstaff.

———— ?¿ ————

Q. What long-time Phoenix newscaster headed the Bola Tie Society and lobbied for "official neckwear" legislation?

A. Bill Close.

———— ?¿ ————

Q. Writer-artist Ross Santee fled New York in 1915 to become a cowboy near what town?

A. Globe.

———— ?¿ ————

Q. Who starred in "The Last Outpost," filmed at Old Tucson in 1951?

A. Ronald Reagan.

———— ?¿ ————

Q. A heroic figure in western garb at Wesley Bolin Plaza celebrates whose memory?

A. Slain lawmen.

Arts and Entertainment

Q. Who was the Belgian baroness whose statue of Father Kino stands in the rotunda of the U.S. Capitol?

A. Suzanne Silvercruys.

————?¿————

Q. What Phoenix kids' show ended in 1989 after a record 35 1/2 years on local TV?

A. "Wallace and Ladmo."

————?¿————

Q. What famous song was first printed in Globe's local newspaper in 1915 as "The Outlaw Broncho"?

A. "Strawberry Roan."

————?¿————

Q. Whose book *Hashknife Cowboy* was judged best non-fiction book of 1984 by the Western Writers of American?

A. Stella Hughes.

————?¿————

Q. What architectural style was used for a number of Santa Fe railroad stations early in the century?

A. Mission Revival.

————?¿————

Q. How much did Hollywood movie makers spend in Arizona in 1989?

A. $34.6 million.

————?¿————

Q. Zane Grey left Arizona in 1929 because the state refused him permission to hunt what big game animal?

A. Bear.

Arts and Entertainment

Q. What location was used for Afghanistan in "Rambo III?"

A. Yuma.

—————— ?¿ ——————

Q. What downtown became 1890s New York for the film "Young Guns II?"

A. Bisbee.

—————— ?¿ ——————

Q. Humorist Dick Wick Hall got national exposure in 1922 when what national magazine reprinted his mimeographed *Salome Sun*?

A. *Saturday Evening Post.*

—————— ?¿ ——————

Q. Who played Cochise in the movies "Broken Arrow" (1950) and "Battle at Apache Pass" (1952)?

A. Jeff Chandler.

—————— ?¿ ——————

Q. What 1966 movie had nothing to do with Arizona's capital, but used the Yuma area as the Arabian desert?

A. "Flight Of The Phoenix."

—————— ?¿ ——————

Q. What German-born artist-naturalist provided records on the Whipple and Ives expeditions of the 1850s?

A. Heinrich Baldwin Mollhausen.

—————— ?¿ ——————

Q. What Zane Grey novel was filmed as a movie at a southern Arizona ranch in 1918?

A. *Light of Western Stars.*

Arts and Entertainment

Q. What is the name of the movie location "town" on the plains northwest of Benson?

A. Mescal.

———?¿———

Q. The 1969 movie "Chastity," filmed in the Phoenix area, starred what husband and wife team?

A. *Sonny and Cher.*

———?¿———

Q. "Stay Away Joe," an Indian stereotype movie filmed at Sedona in 1968, starred who as Joe?

A. Elvis Presley.

———?¿———

Q. What movie tough guy not only made several movies in the Tucson area, but had a home there?

A. Lee Marvin.

———?¿———

Q. Orson Welles, film maker and actor who died in 1985, had a home near what Arizona town?

A. Sedona.

———?¿———

Q. What Oak Creek site, with a backdrop of red stonespires, has probably appeared in more movies than any other Arizona location?

A. Red Rock Crossing.

———?¿———

Q. In what year did *Arizona Highways* run its first color cover?

A. 1937.

Arts and Entertainment

Q. Who took the cover photograph for the December, 1946 *Arizona Highways*, first magazine ever published with color on every page?

A. Barry Goldwater.

———— ?¿ ————

Q. What father and son nature photographers are longtime contributors to *Arizona Highways*?

A. Josef and David Muench.

———— ?¿ ————

Q. What world-famous photographer contributed early black-and-white photos to *Arizona Highways*?

A. Ansel Adams.

———— ?¿ ————

Q. The works of what famous *Life* photographer are collected at the Center For Creative Photography in Tucson?

A. W. Eugene Smith.

———— ?¿ ————

Q. Who was the respected Indian agent who later became editor of the *Tombstone Epitaph*?

A. John P. Clum.

———— ?¿ ————

Q. Gallery of the Sun in the Catalina Foothills celebrates the work of what Arizona-born artist?

A. Ted DeGrazia.

———— ?¿ ————

Q. Who was the correspondent for Harper's who wrote the 1869 book *Adventures In The Apache Country*?

A. J. Ross Browne.

Arts and Entertainment

Q. What publisher-ambassador couple were long-time winter residents of Scottsdale?

A. Henry and Clare Booth Luce.

———————?¿———————

Q. What singer's 1981 tune "Arizona" did the Legislature name an alternate to the obscure state anthem?

A. Rex Allen Jr.

———————?¿———————

Q. What soldier-artist was punished for drawings which now provide an invaluable glimpse of 1848 Arizona?

A. Samuel Chamberlain.

———————?¿———————

Q. How many volumes were in Thomas E. Farish's massive 1915 history of Arizona?

A. Eight.

———————?¿———————

Q. What prestigious private school began in the 1930s as an effort to keep a struggling family ranch solvent?

A. Orme School.

———————?¿———————

Q. What was the professional name of Linda Ronstadt's aunt, a prominent concert singer of the 1930s?

A. Luisa Espinel.

———————?¿———————

Q. What Marty Robbins song won a Grammy in 1960?

A. "El Paso."

Q. While Marty Robbins may be best known for "El Paso," what earlier Robbins hit went gold in 1957?

Arts and Entertainment

A. "A White Sports Coat And A Pink Carnation."

——— ?¿ ———

Q. Who was the Prescott songwriter whose "Sierry Petes" ("Tyin' A Knot In The Devil's Tail") was a cowboy standard?

A. Gail Gardner.

——— ?¿ ———

Q. The facade of what famous church includes bas relief figures of a cat and a mouse?

A. Mission San Xavier del Bac.

——— ?¿ ———

Q. What was the target of Edward Abbey's "The Monkey-Wrench Gang" in his novel of that name?

A. Glen Canyon Dam.

——— ?¿ ———

Q. The annual "Trappings Of The West" show of frontier skills takes place in what city?

A. Flagstaff.

——— ?¿ ———

Q. What's the name of the North Scottsdale Road theme attraction that tries to recreate the Old West?

A. Rawhide.

——— ?¿ ———

Q. What was the ancestral business of rock singer Linda Ronstadt's family?

A. Hardware.

Q. What Maricopa County city now holds an annual celebration featuring ostriches?

Arts and Entertainment

A. Chandler.

————?¿————

Q. What artists' association was organized in a Sedona tavern in 1965?

A. Cowboy Artists of America.

————?¿————

Q. What publisher and philanthropist died in 1929, months before he and his wife were to open a fine museum?

A. Dwight B. Heard.

————?¿————

Q. Who was the draftsman with Kearny's Army of the West who later rendered idealized paintings of 1846 Arizona?

A. John Mix Stanley.

————?¿————

Q. Who was the Tombstone photographer whose works include photos of General Crook and Geronimo negotiating?

A. Camillus S. Fly.

————?¿————

Q. Who was the Arizona ranch woman and teacher who wrote three popular books about teaching in rural schools?

A. Eulalia "Sister" Bourne.

Q. Whose 1889 painting "A Dash For The Timber" was based on two scouting trips through Arizona with soldiers?

A. Frederic Remington.

Arts and Entertainment

Q. Missionary Juan Nentvig's imaginative 1764 description of life in Sonora was called _____ .

A. *Rudo Ensayo*, or "rough essay."

———— ?¿ ————

Q. Arizona State University Professor Rita Dove won a 1987 Pulitzer Prize in what category?

A. Poetry.

———— ?¿ ————

Q. Why did John Waddell's sculptures at the Phoenix Civic Plaza and Maricopa County courthouse offend some people?

A. The figures are nude.

———— ?¿ ————

Q. Apache sculptor Allan Houser's marble "Earth Song" graces the entrance to what Phoenix institution?

A. The Heard Museum.

———— ?¿ ————

Q. What sculptor says his whimsical "Il Donnone" at Phoenix Civic Center represents the ideal relationship between woman and her environment?

A. Paolo Soleri.

———— ?¿ ————

Q. What Scottsdale writer provides the perils for comic strips "Judge Parker," "Rex Morgan, M.D." and "Apartment 3-G?"

A. Nick Dallis.

Q. Gus Arriola, who retired his "Gordo" comic strip in 1985, grew up in what town?

A. Florence.

Q. Who is the popular cartoonist whose long-running "Family Circus" originates from his home in Paradise Valley?

A. Bill Keane.

————?¿————

Q. What syndicated humor columnist writes her tales of domestic comedy from her Phoenix-area home?

A. Erma Bombeck.

————?¿————

Q. What Tucson editorial cartoonist once drew "Sad Sack" comic books?

A. Fred Rhoads.

————?¿————

Q. Who is Tucson's self-styled "amateur" historian who authored more than 25 authoritative books on the Southwest?

A. C.L. Sonnichsen.

————?¿————

Q. Who is the former religion writer who became an authoritative historian of Apache warfare?

A. Dan L. Thrapp.

————?¿————

Q. What annual springtime Tucson festival attracts international musicians?

A. Tucson International Mariachi Conference.

Q. A Disney movie with an Arizona location was called "The Outlaw Cats Of _____ _____?"

A. "Colossal Cave."

Arts and Entertainment

Q. Who was the "Hogan's Heroes" actor slain mysteriously in Scottsdale in 1978?

A. Bob Crane.

———— ?¿ ————

Q. In what ornate courthouse were Barbra Streisand and Kris Kristofferson married in "A Star Is Born?"

A. Pima County (Tucson).

———— ?¿ ————

Q. Who was the Scottsdale TV actress who was a prominent animal rights crusader?

A. Amanda Blake.

———— ?¿ ————

Q. How many people does Grady Gammage Auditorium seat?

A. 3,023.

———— ?¿ ————

Q. Where is Arizona's largest organ, with 2,909 pipes?

A. Grady Gammage Auditorium.

———— ?¿ ————

Q. What famous American artist painted his view of Glen Canyon Dam in the years before his death in 1978?

A. Norman Rockwell.

Q. Payson author Marguerite Noble's popular novel about the hardships of pioneer women was named for what forage plant?

A. *Filaree.*

Arts and Entertainment

Q. Who was hero of a series of silent western movies filmed around Tucson 1913-1915?

A. The Cisco Kid.

————————?¿————————

Q. What group is recognized by a permanent display in the Arizona Hall of Fame Museum?

A. Arizona Women's Hall of Fame.

————————?¿————————

Q. Father Eusebio Francisco Kino is one "Arizonan" in Washington's National Statuary Hall; who's the other?

A. John C. Greenway.

————————?¿————————

Q. What well-known courthouse designer won the competition to design the 1901 Arizona State Capitol?

A. James Riely Gordon.

————————?¿————————

Q. What Payson-area landmark was a refuge for a famous western writer?

A. Zane Grey Lodge.

Q. Who was the author of western novels who posed as a photographer to gain the trust of cowboys?

A. Dane Coolidge.

————————?¿————————

Q. What famed contralto wrote in her memoirs of giving a dusty outdoor concert at Wenden in 1917?

A. Ernestine Schumman-Heink.

Arts and Entertainment

Q. What sometimes-Tucson-based author wrote *Death Wish*, on which the Charles Bronson movie was based?

A. Brian Garfield.

——— ?¿ ———

Q. Jacque Mercer was Arizona's first Miss America in 1949. Who was the second, in 1964?

A. Vonda Kaye Van Dyke.

——— ?¿ ———

Q. Who is the Arizona-born architect whose bold public buildings reflect his Hispanic heritage?

A. Bennie M. Gonzales.

——— ?¿ ———

Q. What dying Tucson artist burned some of his paintings in protest of federal inheritance taxes?

A. Ted DeGrazia.

——— ?¿ ———

Q. Who was the Indian agent and friend of Cochise portrayed by James Stewart in "Broken Arrow?"

A. Tom Jeffords.

Q. Who was the Tucson official who served as studio musician on one of his sister's record albums?

A. Police Chief Peter Ronstadt.

——— ?¿ ———

Q. What 1881 event was the subject of a 1957 movie starring Burt Lancaster and Kirk Douglas?

A. The gunfight at Tombstone's O.K. Corral.

Arts and Entertainment

Q. What was the intended purpose of Frank Lloyd Wright's "Oasis" design, rejected by the Legislature in 1957?

A. A new Arizona state capitol.

———?¿———

Q. What does architect Paolo Soleri call his futuristic city near Cordes Junction?

A. Arcosanti.

———?¿———

Q. What 1985 movie relied heavily on the main street of Florence as a setting for comedy and romance?

A. "Murphy's Romance."

———?¿———

Q. What 1987 TV movie, starring Sam Elliott, was filmed entirely in northern Arizona?

A. "The Quick And The Dead."

———?¿———

Q. Which is best-known of Arizona's several "old time" fiddling contests?

A. The Payson festival.

Q. The father of what rock star operates Chandler's outdoor concert site, Compton Terrace?

A. Stevie Nicks.

———?¿———

Q. What famous American architect established a western base in Arizona in the 1930s?

A. Frank Lloyd Wright.

Arts and Entertainment

Q. What Arizona State University edifice was designed by Frank Lloyd Wright?

A. Grady Gammage Auditorium.

———— ?₂ ————

Q. What long-time Las Vegas singing performer began his career on a Phoenix kids' show?

A. Wayne Newton.

———— ?₂ ————

Q. What book describing family life in Tucson became a 1948 movie starring Dan Dailey and Celeste Holm?

A. *Chicken Every Sunday.*

———— ?₂ ————

Q. How long after his 1967 hit "By The Time I Get To Phoenix" did Glen Campbell move there to live?

A. 14 years.

———— ?₂ ————

Q. What film star was Miss Chevrolet in a 1960 Phoenix auto show?

A. Valerie Perrine.

Q. What Phoenix athlete and actor moved to Los Angeles in 1973 with the William Inge Play "The Last Pad?"

A. Nick Nolte.

———— ?₂ ————

Q. What famous "southern" author spent much of his life in Tucson, then Scottsdale, where he died in 1987?

A. Erskine Caldwell.

Arts and Entertainment

Q. Who's the environmentally active actor who spent his childhood in the Flagstaff area?

A. Ted Danson.

———?¿———

Q. What Tucson-based organization held a national festival there in 1989 to preserve a melodic kind of Americana?

A. The Western Music Association.

———?¿———

Q. What small-town museum boasts a choice collection of work by Frederic Remington and Charles M. Russell?

A. Desert Caballeros Western Museum, Wickenburg.

———?¿———

Q. What New Mexico mystery writer bases his popular novels on the Navajo Tribal Police?

A. Tony Hillerman.

———?¿———

Q. Who was the woman architect who master-planned Fred Harvey installations at the Grand Canyon?

A. Mary Jane Elizabeth Colter.

———?¿———

Q. What famed American artist spent much of his boyhood in Arizona in the 1920s?

A. Jackson Pollock.

———?¿———

Q. Who is a famous American Indian painter who calls Scottsdale home?

A. Fritz Scholder.

Arts and Entertainment

Q. What famed musical comedy was partially filmed near Elgin and Patagonia in southeastern Arizona?

A. "Oklahoma!"

———— ?¿ ————

Q. What classy Phoenix theater, opened in 1929, closed in 1990 for renovation as a historic showplace?

A. The Orpheum.

———— ?¿ ————

Q. Center Stage in Phoenix' Herberger Theater Center seats 800; how many does its Stage West seat?

A. 300.

———— ?¿ ————

Q. What was the cost of Herberger Theater Center by the time it opened in 1989?

A. $19.2 million.

———— ?¿ ————

Q. What birthday did Phoenix Little Theater celebrate in 1990?

A. 70th.

———— ?¿ ————

Q. What arts group overcame traditional rivalry to draw support from patrons in both Phoenix and Tucson?

A. Arizona Opera Company.

———— ?¿ ————

Q. What Hollywood "star" was stranded in a 1927 plane crash into the rugged mountains near Payson?

A. Leo the MGM lion.

Arts and Entertainment

Q. What writer, later an etiquette expert, wrote a motoring guidebook to the West after a daring 1915 trip?

A. Emily Post.

————?¿————

Q. Who was the Arizona song writer who wrote the Tex Ritter hit "Blood On The Saddle?"

A. Romaine Lowdermilk.

————?¿————

Q. What Arizona canyon inspired Gene Autry to write the 1935 tune "Ridin' Down the Canyon?"

A. Oak Creek Canyon.

————?¿————

Q. What all-American movie hero owned two registered Hereford ranches in Arizona?

A. John Wayne.

————?¿————

Q. What famous highway had its own TV series and played a bit part in the 1939 movie "Grapes Of Wrath?"

A. Route 66.

————?¿————

Q. When did KPHO-TV, the first commercial TV station in Arizona, go on the air?

A. 1949.

————?¿————

Q. Who is the Scottsdale author who wrote *Bless the Beasts and Children* and *The Shootist?*

A. Glendon Swarthout.

Arts and Entertainment

Q. What colorful rock star is a graduate of Cortez High School in Phoenix?

A. Alice Cooper.

———— ?ι ————

Q. What TV series was named for the supposed number of Arizona Rangers?

A. "Twenty-six Men."

———— ?ι ————

Q. Who was the Army wife whose book *Vanished Arizona* told vividly of frontier life in 1875?

A. Martha Summerhayes.

———— ?ι ————

Q. Who was the territorial poetess who became an early territorial historian?

A. Sharlot Hall.

———— ?ι ————

Q. What Prescott museum is named for an early Arizona poetess and historian?

A. Sharlot Hall Museum.

———— ?ι ————

Q. Who was the syndicated Arizona cartoonist who won a Pulitzer Prize in 1951 for his Korean War cartoon "Hats?"

A. Reg Manning.

———— ?ι ————

Q. What Phoenix Union High School graduate created World War II GIs Willie and Joe?

A. Cartoonist Bill Mauldin.

Arts and Entertainment

Q. What national radio personality graduated from Phoenix Union High School and started at KOY?

A. Steve Allen.

———?¿———

Q. What were the call letters of Arizona's first licensed commercial radio station in 1922?

A. KFAD (later it became KTAR).

———?¿———

Q. A statue on the courthouse lawn at Prescott commemorates what famous fighting group?

A. Teddy Roosevelt's "Rough Riders."

———?¿———

Q. Who was the World War I flying hero whose statue stands in front of the State Capitol?

A. Frank Luke Jr.

———?¿———

Q. What famous sculptor rendered the Rough Riders statue?

A. Solon Borglum.

Q. A park full of statuary near the Capitol is named for what Arizona governor?

A. Wesley Bolin Plaza.

———?¿———

Q. What two cities have statues of Father Eusebio Francisco Kino?

A. Phoenix and Tucson.

Arts and Entertainment

Q. What is the name of a 1939 Springerville statue honoring pioneer womanhood?

A. "Madonna of the Trail."

———— ?¿ ————

Q. What Zane Grey novel was based on the bloody Pleasant Valley War of the 1880s?

A. *To The Last Man.*

———— ?¿ ————

Q. What canyon was the setting for Zane Grey's 1920s novel *Call Of The Canyon*?

A. Oak Creek Canyon.

———— ?¿ ————

Q. What is the name of architect Frank Lloyd Wright's studio built near Phoenix in 1939?

A. Taliesen West.

———— ?¿ ————

Q. Who was Grady Gammage, for whom Grady Gammage Auditorium was named?

A. President of ASU 1933-59.

LORE & LIES

CHAPTER SEVEN

Q. What Grand Canyon explorer predicted his 1858 expedition would be the last to visit "this profitless locality?"

A. Lieutenant Joseph Christmas Ives.

————?¿————

Q. Henry Wickenburg supposedly found gold in a rock he intended to throw at what?

A. His burro.

————?¿————

Q. Soldiers warned prospector Ed Schieffelin he would find what if he left Camp Huachuca, thereby naming a town?

A. His tombstone.

————?¿————

Q. Before dams trapped silt, what muddy river was called "too thick to swim, too thin to plow?"

A. The Colorado.

————?¿————

Q. Who supposedly said, "We went to war with Mexico to get Arizona and we should go to war with her again to make her take it back?"

A. General William T. Sherman.

145

Lore and Lies

Q. Who was the artist and author who twitted easterners with his mythical Bar X Golf Course?

A. Ross Santee.

———— ?¿ ————

Q. What famed Arizona humorist invented the par-17,000 Greasewood Lynx golf course?

A. Dick Wick Hall.

———— ?¿ ————

Q. What was the nickname for Prescott's first log building?

A. "Fort Misery."

———— ?¿ ————

Q. What was the nickname of mining millionaire James S. Douglas, whose Jerome mansion is now a state park?

A. "Rawhide Jimmy."

———— ?¿ ————

Q. Some Arizona hotels used to advertise free rooms on days which lacked what ingredient?

A. Sunshine.

———— ?¿ ————

Q. What was the motto of the Salome Sun?

A. "Made With A Laugh On A Mimeograph."

———— ?¿ ————

Q. What was Arizona's nickname before Alaska joined the Union?

A. "Baby State."

Lore and Lies

Q. What was the nationality of Jacob Walz, the "Old Dutchman" who supposedly found the Lost Dutchman Mine?

A. German.

———?¿———

Q. What merchandiser caused a national stir in 1938 by selling men's drawers with red ants on them?

A. Barry Goldwater.

———?¿———

Q. Name the fraudulent mine which bilked eastern investors before a newspaperman exposed it in 1898?

A. Spenazuma.

———?¿———

Q. After Florence lobbied for a new bridge across the Gila River in 1885, what happened to the bridge?

A. The river cut a new channel around it.

———?¿———

Q. What hip Phoenix suburb once called itself "The West's Most Western Town"?

A. Scottsdale.

———?¿———

Q. What is the Spanish name of Arizona's best-known ghost, a weeping woman who searches for her dead children?

A. La Llorona.

———?¿———

Q. In what Arizona town did the jail slide 300 feet downhill in 1925, followed closely by the post office?

A. Jerome.

Lore and Lies

Q. What fictional desert varmint combines the features of a jackrabbit and another speedy animal?

A. The Jackalope.

———— ?¿ ————

Q. What city is named for a mythical bird that burned and rose from its own ashes every 500 years?

A. Phoenix.

———— ?¿ ————

Q. What does Spider Woman (who lives on Spider Rock) supposedly do to naughty Navajo children?

A. Eats them.

———— ?¿ ————

Q. What did Cornish miners call the little men who helped them locate ores and warned them of mine cave-ins?

A. Tommyknockers.

———— ?¿ ————

Q. What desert hot spot was once renowned as "Fan Belt Capital of the World?"

A. Gila Bend.

———— ?¿ ————

Q. "The sun shines on Brewery Gulch 330 days in the year, but there is moonshine every night" was the motto of what newspaper?

A. The Brewery Gulch Gazette.

———— ?¿ ————

Q. The name "Tonto" is common among Arizona geographic names. What does it mean in Spanish?

A. "Fool."

Lore and Lies

Q. What northern Arizona town celebrates Groundhog Day with a breakfast including ground hog, i.e. sausage?

A. Snowflake.

————?¿————

Q. What Navajo County woodchopper claimed in 1975 that he was carried away by beings in a flying saucer?

A. Travis Walton.

————?¿————

Q. What Maricopa County town was long known as "Dude Ranch Capital of the World?"

A. Wickenburg.

————?¿————

Q. What former boomtown calls itself "The Town Too Tough To Die?"

A. Tombstone.

————?¿————

Q. What former mining town claims to be the Arizona's liveliest ghost town?

A. Jerome.

————?¿————

Q. What do residents of Why, Arizona say when you ask why Why is called that?

A. "Why not?"

————?¿————

Q. Legend says what happens to people who drink the waters of the Hassayampa River?

A. They never tell the truth again.

Lore and Lies

Q. Dick Wick Hall founded a real town, but peopled it with fictitious characters. What is its name?

A. Salome.

———— ?¿ ————

Q. Will Rogers said of San Carlos Lake, "If this was my lake, I'd mow it." What dam formed the lake?

A. Coolidge Dam.

———— ?¿ ————

Q. What was the hometown of the seven-year-old frog who never learned to swim?

A. Salome.

———— ?¿ ————

Q. According to an old Tucson gag, at what temperature does the ice break up on the Santa Cruz River each spring?

A. 100 degrees Fahrenheit.

———— ?¿ ————

Q. What famous guide and storyteller claimed he built the San Francisco Peaks with dirt from the Grand Canyon?

A. John "Cap" Hance.

———— ?¿ ————

Q. Dick Wick Hall fancied that a scorpion was the desert version of what oceanic creature?

A. Lobster.

———— ?¿ ————

Q. What part-time Arizona resident said, "What this country needs is a good five-cent cigar?"

A. Vice President Thomas R. Marshall.

Lore and Lies

Q. What was the other name of Charles A. Franklin, yarn spinner who helped create Apache County?

A. Albert Franklin Banta.

————?¿————

Q. Whose fanciful reports of golden cities spurred the huge Coronado expedition of 1540?

A. Fray Marcos de Niza.

————?¿————

Q. What pioneer told a fanciful story of trading a lot in a new townsite for a ferry ride across the Colorado River?

A. Charles D. Poston.

————?¿————

Q. What kind of animal was Red Ghost, who roamed Arizona with a human skeleton strapped to his back?

A. A camel.

————?¿————

Q. What Pinal County whistle-stop was the seat of James Addison Reavis' fictitious Barony of Arizona?

A. Arizola.

————?¿————

Q. What is the name of the fabled White Mountains gold cache that eluded searchers in the 1860s?

A. The Lost Adams Diggings.

————?¿————

Q. What explorer traveled the Colorado River in 1605 and started a rumor that California was an island?

A. Juan de Onate.

Lore and Lies

Q. Cap Hance liked to tell dudes of snowshoeing across Grand Canyon on winter nights when what froze over?

A. Fog.

SCIENCE & NATURE

C H A P T E R   E I G H T

Q. Where were the 225-million-year-old remains of "Gertie," the earliest dinosaur known, found in 1984?

A. Petrified Forest National Park.

————?¿————

Q. What dry southern Arizona cave preserved evidence of humans there 10,000 years ago?

A. Ventana Cave.

————?¿————

Q. Three types of desert in Arizona are labeled Sonoran, Mojave and _____.

A. Chihuahuan.

————?¿————

Q. What southwest Arizona region beguiled naturalists long before it became an 860,000-acre national widlife refuge in 1939?

A. Cabeza Prieta.

————?¿————

Q. At what village is the Southwest Research Station of the American Museum of Natural History?

A. Portal.

Science and Nature

Q. What internationally known naturalist, turned Tucsonan, wrote *The Voice of the Desert* and *Grand Canyon?*

A. Joseph Wood Krutch.

———— ?¿ ————

Q. What was the highest temperature ever recorded in Arizona?

A. 127°F.

———— ?¿ ————

Q. What was the Phoenix temperature June 26, 1990, highest ever recorded there?

A. 122°F.

———— ?¿ ————

Q. What was the greatest accumulation of snow ever recorded in Phoenix?

A. 1 inch.

———— ?¿ ————

Q. What was the heaviest rain reported in Phoenix in a 24-hour period?

A. 4.98 inches (1911).

———— ?¿ ————

Q. What was the lowest temperature ever recorded in Phoenix?

A. 16°F.

———— ?¿ ————

Q. What was Arizona's heaviest snowfall from one storm?

A. 67 inches (Heber, 1967).

Q. Where was Arizona's greatest snowfall in one season, 400.9 inches?

A. Hawley Lake.

————?¿————

Q. What was Arizona's heaviest reported rainfall in 24 hours?

A. 11.40 inches (Workman Creek, 1970).

————?¿————

Q. Where was a rainfall of 5.3 inches measured during 70 minutes on July 11, 1878?

A. Tucson.

————?¿————

Q. In Los Angeles and Miami, the sun shines 73 percent of the possible time; what is the figure for Tucson?

A. 86 percent.

————?¿————

Q. What is the average maximum temperature in Phoenix in July?

A. 107°F.

————?¿————

Q. How much cooler does Tucson average in summer than Phoenix?

A. Six degrees.

————?¿————

Q. What's the average minimum temperature in Phoenix in December and January?

A. 44°F.

Science and Nature

Q. What's the earliest date the Phoenix temperature reached 100 degrees?

A. March 26 (1988).

———— ?¿ ————

Q. What was the latest date that Phoenix had its first 100-degree reading?

A. June 18 (1913).

———— ?¿ ————

Q. What Colorado River towns sometimes "compete" for the nation's highest temperatures?

A. Bullhead City and Lake Havasu City.

———— ?¿ ————

Q. Winslow is noted as a railroad town and for what weather phenomenon?

A. Strong winds.

———— ?¿ ————

Q. The driest weather ever recorded in Arizona was in 1956 when only 0.07 inch of rain fell at what location?

A. Davis Dam (Bullhead City).

———— ?¿ ————

Q. What location received the greatest amount of precipitation in one year, 58.92 inches in 1978?

A. Hawley Lake.

———— ?¿ ————

Q. Annual rainfall on some Arizona deserts is less than 3 inches; what is the average in the White Mountains?

A. More than 30 inches.

Science and Nature

Q. What is the average annual amount of precipitation at Phoenix?

A. 7.01 inches.

——————?¿——————

Q. What was Arizona's lowest recorded temperature at Hawley Lake January 7, 1971?

A. -40°F.

——————?¿——————

Q. What is the name of the reptile that seems to have a fancy beaded hide?

A. Gila monster.

——————?¿——————

Q. What central Phoenix museum is internationally respected as an anthropological showcase?

A. The Heard Museum.

——————?¿——————

Q. What is Arizona's official state fossil?

A. Petrified wood.

——————?¿——————

Q. What innovative "zoo" has underground chambers showing how wild creatures hole up during hot afternoons?

A. The Arizona-Sonora Desert Museum.

——————?¿——————

Q. What Boston brahmin and scientist established an astronomical observatory at Flagstaff in 1893-94?

A. Percival Lowell.

Science and Nature

Q. What planet was discovered from Lowell Observatory in 1930?

A. Pluto.

————— ?¿ —————

Q. What observatory sits atop a peak west of Tucson?

A. Kitt Peak National Observatory.

————— ?¿ —————

Q. How many species of tree squirrels are native to Arizona?

A. Nine.

————— ?¿ —————

Q. What endangered species of squirrel triggered a national environmental flap in 1990?

A. Mount Graham red squirrel.

————— ?¿ —————

Q. What year did Northern Arizona University's forestry school graduate its first class?

A. 1961.

————— ?¿ —————

Q. Where do "blowholes" vent air periodically to equalize surface and subterranean air pressure?

A. Wupatki National Monument.

————— ?¿ —————

Q. "Apache Tears" are what kind of stone?

A. Obsidian.

————— ?¿ —————

Q. What strain of Spanish horses has retained pure blood lines on a remote Arivaca ranch since 1885?

A. Mustangs.

————?i————

Q. The U.S. Geological Survey established what branch at Flagstaff to help find landing sites on the moon?

A. Astrogeology.

————?i————

Q. What desert flower blooms in the dark of summer nights?

A. Night-blooming cereus.

————?i————

Q. At Petrified Forest, what is the name of the seven-room prehistoric pueblo made entirely of petrified wood?

A. Agate House.

————?i————

Q. The Smithsonian Institution's optical observatory is located on what peak south of Tucson?

A. Mount Hopkins.

————?i————

Q. What is the Spanish name of a high-country shrub whose branches are gnarled and shiny red?

A. Manzanita ("little apple").

————?i————

Q. What kind of cactus is so treacherous that it is falsely called "jumping cactus?"

A. Cholla.

————?i————

Q. What kind of desert plant is also called "Spanish dagger?"

Science and Nature

A. Yucca.

———— ?¿ ————

Q. Needles of the ponderosa pine come grouped in "bundles" of how many?

A. Three.

———— ?¿ ————

Q. What conifer produces a tiny nut gathered and sold by the pound?

A. Pinyon.

———— ?¿ ————

Q. What is the most common type of juniper in Arizona?

A. Utah juniper.

———— ?¿ ————

Q. What kind of juniper has ragged bark scored in rectangular plates?

A. Alligator juniper.

———— ?¿ ————

Q. What kind of fish was the "white salmon" once reported to grow to 100 pounds in Arizona waters?

A. Squawfish.

———— ?¿ ————

Q. How many rattlesnake species are native to Arizona?

A. 3 (17 subspecies).

———— ?¿ ————

Q. The western diamondback rattlesnake accounts for approximately how many deaths a year in Arizona?

A. One.

Science and Nature

Q. How many kinds of lizard are native to Arizona?
A. 43.

———?¿———

Q. How many species of bird are native to Arizona?
A. 475.

———?¿———

Q. What handsome, top-knotted species of quail is most familiar in Arizona?
A. Gambel's.

———?¿———

Q. With 28 species lurking about, Arizona is rated one of the top states in the nation for what kind of mammal?
A. Bats.

———?¿———

Q. How many species of hummingbird are found in Arizona?
A. 16.

———?¿———

Q. What fish was named Arizona's official state fish by the 1986 Legislature?
A. Apache or Native trout.

———?¿———

Q. What is the state's official amphibian?
A. Arizona tree frog.

———?¿———

Q. The agave or "century plant" blooms at what interval?
A. 25 years.

Science and Nature

Q. What cactus-like shrub is reminiscent of a cluster of coach whips?

A. Ocotillo.

——— ?¿ ———

Q. What low-growing shrub usually looks like a weed, but blooms golden across vast stretches in the fall?

A. Golden Rabbitbrush.

——— ?¿ ———

Q. What's a common name for tamarisk, which grows along Arizona streambeds?

A. Salt Cedar.

——— ?¿ ———

Q. The oak tree which grows in dense groves among ponderosa pine is called what?

A. Gambel Oak.

——— ?¿ ———

Q. What native species of elk was extinct in Arizona by 1900?

A. Merriam elk.

——— ?¿ ———

Q. What kind of elk was imported into Arizona in 1913 and now thrives?

A. Wapiti.

——— ?¿ ———

Q. Two federal game preserves protect what kind of rare wild sheep?

A. Desert bighorns.

Science and Nature

Q. The grizzly bear became extinct in Arizona in 1916; what bear still lives in the state?

A. Black bear.

—————?¿—————

Q. What small mammal travels in packs of 40 or 50 through the high grasslands of southeastern Arizona?

A. Coatamundi.

—————?¿—————

Q. The 1904 invention that looks like a satellite dish in historic photos was actually what?

A. A solar-powered water pump.

—————?¿—————

Q. What canyon on the west side of the Kofa mountains contains a few of the rare palm trees native to Arizona?

A. Palm Canyon.

—————?¿—————

Q. What botanical garden, founded by an early mining magnate, has recently become an Arizona state park?

A. Boyce Thompson Arboretum.

—————?¿—————

Q. What animal lies dormant in desert soil, emerging only after torrential summer rains?

A. The spadefoot toad.

—————?¿—————

Q. Arizona's most severe earthquake in 1887 centered where?

A. Near Fronteras, Mexico.

Science and Nature

Q. What natural cause, triggered by the Sonoran Earthquake of 1887, closed Tombstone's famous silver mines?

A. Water.

——— ?¿ ———

Q. What new crop is being cultivated at exotic farms all along the Gila River basin in central Arizona?

A. Fish.

——— ?¿ ———

Q. What non-native beast has been raised in northern Arizona since 1927 to help prevent its extinction?

A. Bison.

——— ?¿ ———

Q. The Mile Hi/Ramsey Canyon Preserve draws "birders" to a canyon in what mountain range?

A. Huachuca.

——— ?¿ ———

Q. Name the controlled environment near Oracle which eight people entered in 1990 for a two-year stay?

A. Biosphere II.

——— ?¿ ———

Q. The Russian thistle is a pesky plant more commonly known as what?

A. Tumbleweed.

——— ?¿ ———

Q. What Tucson installation pioneered hydroponics and desalinization of seawater in arid nations?

A. Environmental Research Laboratory.

Science and Nature

Q. In what canyon east of Flagstaff did the vanished Sinagua simply wall up rock overhangs to create dwellings?

A. Walnut Canyon.

—————?¿—————

Q. What practice of the vanished Hohokam has made it difficult for archaeologists to study them?

A. They cremated their dead.

—————?¿—————

Q. Buenos Aires National Wildlife Refuge was established in 1985 to preserve what endangered bird?

A. Masked bobwhite quail.

—————?¿—————

Q. Havasu National Wildlife Refuge includes what picturesque river canyon?

A. Topock Gorge.

—————?¿—————

Q. What is the name of the caverns which yielded the remains of a 20,000-year-old ground sloth?

A. Grand Canyon Caverns.

—————?¿—————

Q. What kind of tree is Arizona's oldest, estimated at more than 1,400 years of age?

A. Bristlecone pine.

—————?¿—————

Q. What astronomy-trained scientist invented tree-ring dating for archaeological sites?

A. Dr. A.E. Douglas.

Science and Nature

Q. What diminutive, feathered creature is threatened by extinction in Arizona's dwindling woodlands?

A. The Mexican spotted owl.

———— ?¿ ————

Q. What Colorado River area north of Yuma seeks to save bird and mammal habitats destroyed elsewhere by dams?

A. Imperial National Wildlife Refuge.

———— ?¿ ————

Q. What fragile, threatened type of woodland is the Nature Conservacy preserving on the Hassayampa River?

A. A cottonwood-willow forest.

———— ?¿ ————

Q. What four-footed wild creature is adapting to Arizona cities?

A. The coyote.

———— ?¿ ————

Q. What homely wild pig, once reclusive, has begun encroaching on small-town gardens and garbage cans?

A. The peccary or javelina.

———— ?¿ ————

Q. How many people were employed in astronomy in Arizona according to a 1988 study?

A. 1,000.

———— ?¿ ————

Q. Where is the McMath Solar Telescope, largest in the world?

A. Kitt Peak National Observatory.

Science and Nature

Q. What institution has collected 1,300 visitors from space?

A. ASU's Center for Meteorite Studies.

———————?¿———————

Q. The cacti specimens at what Phoenix garden represent more than half the world's 5,000 identified species?

A. Desert Botanical Garden.

———————?¿———————

Q. How tall is the world's tallest saguaro as recognized by the *Guiness Book of World Records?*

A. 57 feet 11 3/4 inches.

———————?¿———————

Q. What year did Dr. Willys Carrier, inventor of air conditioning, refrigerate a mine near Superior?

A. 1937.

———————?¿———————

Q. Everyone says Arizona has a certain kind of heat, and it's backed by scientific fact. What kind is it?

A. "Dry heat."

———————?¿———————

Q. What region's intense thunderstorms, first noted by General George Crook in 1871, were confirmed by scientists?

A. The Mogollon Rim.

———————?¿———————

Q. Birdwatchers visit canyons in what southeastern Arizona range in hopes of seeing the Elegant Trogon?

A. The Chiricahuas.

Science and Nature

Q. What bird nests only in cavities in saguaros?

A. The elf owl.

———— ?¿ ————

Q. Which of the Apollo astronauts was reared in Tucson?

A. Frank Borman.

———— ?¿ ————

Q. Northern Arizona has the world's largest stand of what species of pine?

A. Ponderosa.

———— ?¿ ————

Q. Astronauts trained for the moon landing in cinder fields near what Arizona city?

A. Flagstaff.

———— ?¿ ————

Q. What common desert tree produces long bean pods, once a food staple for Native Americans?

A. Mesquite.

———— ?¿ ————

Q. What heavenly objects, now in the Smithsonian Institution, formed anvils for early Tucsonians?

A. Meteorite fragments.

———— ?¿ ————

Q. What is the name of Flagstaff's respected anthropological museum?

A. The Museum of Northern Arizona.

———— ?¿ ————

Q. What graceful, nearly-extinct animal was bred in captivity at the Phoenix Zoo during the 1960s?

A. The Arabian oryx.

————?¿————

Q. Three rare cubs were born at the Phoenix Zoo in the spring of 1990. What kind are they?

A. Sumatran tiger.

————?¿————

Q. What winter visitor from Canada nests along the lower Colorado River?

A. Snow goose.

————?¿————

Q. What raucous, colorful bird keeps a close eye on campers in northern Arizona forests?

A. Stellar's jay.

————?¿————

Q. What kind of plant is preserved in a two-part national monument located both east and west of Tucson?

A. The saguaro cactus.

————?¿————

Q. What national monument south of Ajo celebrates a graceful cactus, reminiscent of religious music?

A. Organ Pipe Cactus National Monument.

————?¿————

Q. What kind of plant is commemorated by a "parkway" along U.S. 93 northwest of Wickenburg?

A. Joshua Tree.

————?¿————

Q. What picturesque desert bird is a member of the cuckoo family?

Science and Nature

A. The roadrunner.

———— ?¿ ————

Q. What discipline drew Captain John G. Bourke to study the Indians of the Southwest in the 19th Century?

A. "Ethnology," or anthropology.

POLITICS & GOVERNMENT

CHAPTER NINE

Q. What Arizona governor served seven intermittent terms between 1912 and 1932?

A. George W.P. Hunt.

———?¿———

Q. Who was the only person to serve as U.S. Senator, Arizona supreme court justice and governor?

A. Ernest W. McFarland.

———?¿———

Q. Who was the first Arizonan appointed to the U.S. Supreme Court?

A. Chief Justice William H. Rehnquist.

———?¿———

Q. What Arizona judge was the first woman appointed to the U.S. Supreme Court?

A. Sandra Day O'Connor.

———?¿———

Q. What member of a pioneer Arizona Mormon family was interior secretary during the Kennedy administration?

A. Stewart L. Udall.

Politics and Government

Q. What Arizona justice was the first woman chief justice of any state supreme court?

A. Lorna Lockwood.

———— ?¿ ————

Q. Who was Arizona's first woman governor?

A. Rose Mofford.

———— ?¿ ————

Q. Who was the former sheriff who served a combined 56 1/2 years in the U.S. House of Representatives and Senate?

A. Carl Hayden.

———— ?¿ ————

Q. Who was Arizona's first woman U.S. Representative, elected in 1934?

A. Isabella Greenway.

———— ?¿ ————

Q. What Arizona territorial governor has been called "The Pathfinder Of The West?"

A. John C. Fremont.

———— ?¿ ————

Q. Which Arizona governor persuaded voters to abolish capital punishment in 1916?

A. George W. P. Hunt.

———— ?¿ ————

Q. Who was the U.S. senator from Indiana who worked diligently to block Arizona's admission to the Union?

A. Albert Beveridge.

Politics and Government

Q. Governor Richard E. Sloan and his family were homeless after what Phoenix landmark burned May 17, 1910?

A. Hotel Adams.

―――――?¿―――――

Q. What pioneer suffragette and woman's rights advocate became Arizona's first female state senator?

A. Frances Willard Munds.

―――――?¿―――――

Q. What year did male voters favor woman suffrage in Arizona by a 2-1 margin?

A. 1912.

―――――?¿―――――

Q. Why couldn't John A. Gurley, appointed first governor of Arizona Territory, fill the post?

A. He died in Washington, D.C.

―――――?¿―――――

Q. Who was the first woman elected to the Arizona House of Representatives?

A. Rachel Berry.

―――――?¿―――――

Q. After capital punishment was abolished in 1916, how long was it before voters reinstated the death penalty?

A. Two years.

―――――?¿―――――

Q. Who was the state senator licensed to operate both airplanes and steamboats?

A. Nellie T. Bush.

Politics and Government

Q. Besides serving in Congress, Isabella C. Greenway owned what posh Tucson resort?

A. Arizona Inn.

———— ?¿ ————

Q. Who helped dedicate Tucson's restored Fremont House in 1972?

A. First lady Pat Nixon.

———— ?¿ ————

Q. Who was the planned-parenthood crusader who operated from Tucson between 1934 and her death in 1966?

A. Margaret Sanger.

———— ?¿ ————

Q. What disgruntled 1958 gubernatorial candidate started *The Arizona Journal* in 1962?

A. Robert Morrison.

———— ?¿ ————

Q. What state park, housed in an 1878 adobe courthouse, holds the papers of a one-time U.S. Senate majority leader?

A. McFarland State Park, Florence.

———— ?¿ ————

Q. In 1871 a leading candidate shot the other and the dark-horse candidate won what office?

A. Maricopa County Sheriff.

———— ?¿ ————

Q. What was former Attorney General Robert Morrison's Armenian name before he had it legally changed in 1942?

A. Berj Mosekian.

Politics and Government

Q. What Roosevelt and her husband founded the short-lived *Arizona Times* in Phoenix in 1946?

A. Anna Roosevelt Boettiger, daughter of FDR.

————?₂————

Q. Other states signed the Colorado River Compact in 1922, but Arizona did not ratify it until when?

A. 1944.

————?₂————

Q. The legislature's longest filibuster, 22 hours in 1944, sought to block a vote on what measure?

A. Ratification of the Colorado River Compact.

————?₂————

Q. When did the U.S. Supreme Court exclude Gila River water from Arizona's Colorado River allocation?

A. 1963.

————?₂————

Q. When did President Lyndon Johnson sign the bill authorizing construction of the Central Arizona Project?

A. 1968.

————?₂————

Q. What census qualified Arizona for a second seat in the U.S. House of Representatives?

A. 1940.

————?₂————

Q. What Arizona senator was acting vice president following the assassination of John F. Kennedy?

A. Carl Hayden, Senate president pro-tempore.

Politics and Government

Q. The Kent Decree of 1910 affirmed what ruling principal for Arizona water rights?

A. "Prior appropriation."

———— ?¿ ————

Q. Who was elected Arizona Territory's first non-voting delegate to Congress?

A. Charles D. Poston.

———— ?¿ ————

Q. What year were older portions of the Capitol replaced by the nine-story "west wing"?

A. 1974.

———— ?¿ ————

Q. After U.S. Representative Stewart L. Udall became Interior Secretary in 1961, who was elected to replace him in Congress?

A. His brother Morris K. Udall.

———— ?¿ ————

Q. What year did Arizona's ardent prohibitionists finally succeed in having the state voted dry?

A. 1916.

Q. Who was Arizona's first four-year governor after terms were extended from two years in 1968?

A. Jack Williams.

———— ?¿ ————

Q. How many secretaries of state have succeeded to the governorship?

A. Three.

Politics and Government

Q. Who is the only Arizona attorney general to succeed to the governorship?

A. Bruce Babbitt.

———————?¿———————

Q. What early secretary of state and long-time aspirant to the governor's chair finally made it in 1940?

A. Sidney P. Osborn.

———————?¿———————

Q. What one-term governor used the roadrunner as his campaign symbol in an earlier try for the office?

A. Sam Goddard, 1965-66.

———————?¿———————

Q. The Arizona state lottery was inaugurated July 1 of what year?

A. 1981.

———————?¿———————

Q. What year was Arizona's antimiscegenation law repealed?

A. 1962.

———————?¿———————

Q. Teddy Roosevelt appointed which of his former Rough Rider captains to be governor of Arizona Territory?

A. Alexander O. Brodie.

———————?¿———————

Q. Who was the woman who missed being elected governor of Arizona by fewer than 3,000 votes in 1950?

A. Ana Frohmiller.

Politics and Government

Q. In the 1964 presidential election, how many Arizona counties did Barry Goldwater carry?

A. Four.

——— ?¿ ———

Q. What was the flowing middle name of U.S. Senator Henry F. Ashurst?

A. Fountain.

——— ?¿ ———

Q. President Taft vetoed Arizona's statehood until what provision was deleted from the constitution?

A. Recall of judges.

——— ?¿ ———

Q. Who was the first Oriental legislator in Arizona in 1947?

A. Representative Wing F. Ong.

——— ?¿ ———

Q. Who was Arizona's first woman office holder beginning in 1909?

A. Territorial Historian Sharlot Hall.

——— ?¿ ———

Q. Who was the first black legislator in Arizona in 1951?

A. Carl Sims Jr.

——— ?¿ ———

Q. Who served eight terms as territorial delegate to Congress, eight years as U.S. senator after statehood?

A. Marcus Aurelius Smith.

——— ?¿ ———

Q. Name two former state supreme court justices born of different mothers but with the same polygamous father.

Politics and Government

A. Jesse A. and Levi S. Udall.

―――――?ا―――――

Q. Who was the first black elected to the Arizona State Senate?

A. Clovis Campbell (1962).

―――――?ا―――――

Q. Following a close election in 1916, George W.P. Hunt refused to relinquish the governor's office to whom?

A. Thomas E. Campbell.

―――――?ا―――――

Q. Who was the Arizona governor who unsuccessfully sought the Democratic presidential nomination in 1988?

A. Bruce Babbitt.

―――――?ا―――――

Q. What liberal Arizona congressman, known for his folksy wit, sought the Democratic nomination for president in 1976?

A. Morris K. Udall.

―――――?ا―――――

Q. What recent Phoenix mayor is the son of an Arizona governor from the 1960s?

A. Terry Goddard.

―――――?ا―――――

Q. What U.S. vice president called Scottsdale home during the winter months?

A. Thomas Riley Marshall.

―――――?ا―――――

Q. The late Dr. and Mrs. Royal Davis of Phoenix were the parents of what U.S. First Lady?

Politics and Government

A. Nancy Reagan.

———— ?¿ ————

Q. What former Arizona congressman was appointed U.S. Ambassador to Great Britain in 1947?

A. Lewis W. Douglas.

———— ?¿ ————

Q. What Arizona governor was removed from office by the State Senate after an impeachment trial in 1988?

A. Evan Mecham.

———— ?¿ ————

Q. What former Arizona governor served as U.S. Ambassador to El Salvador, Bolivia and Argentina?

A. Raul Castro.

———— ?¿ ————

Q. What former Phoenix department store executive ran for President in 1964?

A. U.S. Senator Barry Goldwater.

———— ?¿ ————

Q. Which of Arizona's governors was born in Mexico?

A. Raul Castro.

———— ?¿ ————

Q. Barry M. Goldwater's middle name, Morris, is from an uncle who was a leader in what political party?

A. Arizona Democratic party.

———— ?¿ ————

Q. Which two former Arizona governors were popular radio personalities before they went into politics?

A. Howard Pyle and Jack Williams.

SPORTS & LEISURE

CHAPTER TEN

Q. What conference did Arizona State University and the University of Arizona leave in 1978 to join the Pacific 10?

A. Western Athletic Conference.

———— ?¿ ————

Q. What winning 1950s football coach won 27, lost 3 in his brief career at Arizona State?

A. Dan Devine (1955-57).

———— ?¿ ————

Q. Who was the construction magnate who owned the New York Yankees for 20 seasons?

A. Del Webb.

———— ?¿ ————

Q. Mickey Mantle started his rookie year in Arizona (1950) because the Yankees swapped training sites with whom?

A. New York Giants.

———— ?¿ ————

Q. What former ASU slugger was National League Rookie of the Year in 1978?

A. Bob Horner.

Sports and Leisure

Q. What Phoenix Sun scored 60 points in a game against Seattle in 1990?

A. Tom Chambers.

——— ?¿ ———

Q. What is the name of the 51-mile-long foot trail that gives hikers access to the base of the Mogollon Rim?

A. Highline Trail.

——— ?¿ ———

Q. What was the weight of the largest catfish ever reported by an Arizona fisherman?

A. 65 pounds.

——— ?¿ ———

Q. Which pro golfers have won the Phoenix open three times each?

A. Gene Littler, Arnold Palmer.

——— ?¿ ———

Q. Who was the small, powerful golfer who won the Phoenix Open in 1946 and repeated in 1947?

A. Ben Hogan.

——— ?¿ ———

Q. Larry Kendall, who coached Arizona's baseball team to four championships, played on what championship team?

A. Minnesota, 1956.

——— ?¿ ———

Q. What ASU placekicker set five NCAA records?

A. Luis Zendejas.

Sports and Leisure

Q. The biggest fish taken by an Arizona fisherman from the Colorado River weighed 59 pounds. What kind was it?

A. Striped bass.

———— ?¿ ————

Q. What southern Arizona high schools claim the nation's second-oldest football rivalry, 125 games in 84 years?

A. Douglas and Bisbee.

———— ?¿ ————

Q. What nationally-ranked women's softball catcher switched to bowling in 1962 and promptly won the WIBC title?

A. Dot Wilkinson.

———— ?¿ ————

Q. What Phoenix race driver won at Le Mans in 1957 and Indianapolis in 1958?

A. Jimmy Bryan.

———— ?¿ ————

Q. Dick Van Arsdale, first Phoenix Sun chosen in the 1968 NBA expansion draft, retired with how many points?

A. 15,079.

———— ?¿ ————

Q. What Phoenix driver was Rookie of the Year in the Indy 500 in 1951?

A. Bobby Ball.

———— ?¿ ————

Q. New York Giants pitcher Art Nehf, a member of the Arizona Sports Hall of Fame, played in how many World Series?

A. Four, 1921 to 1924.

Q. How many gold medals did ASU football great Henry Carr win in the 1964 Olympics?

A. Two (220 meters, 1,600 meters).

——— ?¿ ———

Q. What former Kingman High School star played in the famous Chicago Cubs infield of 1923-24?

A. George Farley Grantham.

——— ?¿ ———

Q. In what event did Dallas Long of Phoenix set a national record in 1958 and win an Olympic gold medal in 1960?

A. Shot put.

——— ?¿ ———

Q. How many first-round NFL draft choices came from the U of A in 1990?

A. Two (Chris Singleton, Anthony Smith).

——— ?¿ ———

Q. What record-breaking runner was victim of a Phoenix car-pedestrian accident while training for the 1984 Olympics?

A. Kathy Gibbons Jackson.

——— ?¿ ———

Q. How many field goals per game did Alvin Adams average in 13 seasons with the Phoenix Suns?

A. 14.

——— ?¿ ———

Q. What Phoenix Sun scored 14 field goals and six free throws without a miss in a 1983 game against Seattle?

A. Walter Davis.

Sports and Leisure

Q. How many golf courses did the Arizona Golfing Association list in its 1990 directory?

A. 204.

———— ?¿ ————

Q. What Arizona congressman played one season for the Denver Nuggets of the NBL?

A. Morris K. Udall.

———— ?¿ ————

Q. What was the name of the downtown sports arena that served Phoenix for more than 40 years?

A. Madison Square Garden.

———— ?¿ ————

Q. What legendary ASU football coach lost his job after 22 seasons because of allegations that he abused a player?

A. Frank Kush.

———— ?¿ ————

Q. The late, fiery manager Billy Martin once played third base for the Phoenix Senators in what Class C league?

A. Arizona-Texas League.

———— ?¿ ————

Q. In what class was the Arizona State League, a baseball circuit that brought joy to mining towns in 1928?

A. Class D.

———— ?¿ ————

Q. Michael Carbajal of Phoenix, who won an Olympic gold medal in 1988, won what championship in 1990?

A. International Boxing Association's flyweight title.

Sports and Leisure

Q. Mesa athlete Jay Barrs won a gold medal in the 1988 Olympics in what sport?

A. Archery.

——— ?¿ ———

Q. How many years did the Cardinals professional football team play in St. Louis before moving to Phoenix in 1988?

A. 28.

——— ?¿ ———

Q. What former Phoenix Suns star coached Grand Canyon College to a national basketball title in 1987-88?

A. Paul Westphal.

——— ?¿ ———

Q. Phoenix became the only U.S. city currently on what racing circuit 1989-1993?

A. Formula One Grand Prix.

——— ?¿ ———

Q. What two teams were matched in both the 1988 and 1990 Fiesta Bowl games?

A. Florida State and Nebraska.

——— ?¿ ———

Q. Arizona State College, now ASU, adopted the nickname "Sun Devils" in 1946; what was ASC's earlier nickname?

A. Bulldogs.

——— ?¿ ———

Q. The Phoenix Firebirds are the top farm team of what major league club?

A. New York Giants.

Q. Sun Devil Stadium, site of the 1993 Super Bowl, seats how many people?

A. 74,864.

———— ?ᵢ ————

Q. What team did Notre Dame defeat 34-21 in the 1989 Fiesta Bowl to win the national football title?

A. West Virginia.

———— ?ᵢ ————

Q. The first time a national title was decided in the Fiesta Bowl was when Penn State beat Miami in what year?

A. 1987.

———— ?ᵢ ————

Q. The long-time Phoenix Giants of the Pacific Coast League changed their name to what in 1985?

A. Firebirds.

———— ?ᵢ ————

Q. What Tempe amusement park installed a wave machine to capitalize on a 1960s California craze?

A. Big Surf.

———— ?ᵢ ————

Q. The Phoenix Roadrunners played what kind of professional sport from 1967 to 1979?

A. Hockey.

———— ?ᵢ ————

Q. The Tucson Astros of the Class AAA Pacific Coast League were known by what name until 1980?

A. The Tucson Toros.

Sports and Leisure

A. 1965.

———— ?¿ ————

Q. America West Arena scheduled to open in Phoenix in 1992 was designed to seat how many?

A. 19,394.

———— ?¿ ————

Q. The America West Arena sits on the site of what historic landmark?

A. Phoenix Fire Station No. 1.

———— ?¿ ————

Q. What peak in the Phoenix Mountains Preserve draws hundreds of hikers daily?

A. Squaw Peak.

———— ?¿ ————

Q. How far did Mike Secrest of Scottsdale pedal his bicycle in April, 1990, for a new world 24-hour record?

A. 1,216 miles.

———— ?¿ ————

Q. What surface did early Arizona golf courses use in lieu of grass?

A. Oiled sand.

———— ?¿ ————

Q. What was Byron Nelson's purse for winning the 1939 Phoenix Open golf tournament?

A. $700.

———— ?¿ ————

Q. What businessman did fellow Phoenix Thunderbirds dub "Father of the Phoenix Open?"

A. Bob Goldwater.

Sports and Leisure

Q. Former Round Valley High School and New York Jets football player Mark Gastineau switched to what sport in 1990?

A. Boxing.

———— ?¿ ————

Q. How many major league baseball teams come to Arizona for spring training in the "Cactus League?"

A. Eight.

———— ?¿ ————

Q. What major league team has trained in Tucson each spring since 1947?

A. The Cleveland Indians.

———— ?¿ ————

Q. Who introduced "spring training" to Arizona in 1927 when he showed off his skills near the Phoenix railroad depot?

A. Babe Ruth.

———— ?¿ ————

Q. Rose Mofford, Arizona's first woman governor, once rejected a contract to play what pro sport?

A. Women's basketball.

———— ?¿ ————

Q. What Hillside rancher was first president of the Cowboys Turtle Association, (now Professional Rodeo Cowboys Association)?

A. Everett Bowman.

———— ?¿ ————

Q. What Baltimore Oriole, a three-time Cy Young Award winner, was all-state in baseball, basketball and football at Scottdale High School?

Sports and Leisure

A. Jim Palmer.

——— ?¿ ———

Q. What fieldhouse allows indoor football and other sports in Flagstaff's wintery weather?

A. Northern Arizona University's Walkup Skydome.

——— ?¿ ———

Q. What famed black athlete became an active community leader in Phoenix in his later life?

A. Jesse Owens.

——— ?¿ ———

Q. What four-year college in Phoenix, with a bright record in small-college sports, is now a university?

A. Grand Canyon University.

——— ?¿ ———

Q. What did diminutive Hopi runner Lewis Tewanima bring home from the 1912 Olympic games in Stockholm?

A. A silver medal for the 10,000-meter run.

——— ?¿ ———

Q. Who was Arizona's first Olympic gold medal winner, a member of the 400-meter relay team at the 1928 Amsterdam games?

A. Charles Borah.

——— ?¿ ———

Q. What rodeo has registered the trademark "World's Oldest Rodeo" because the show dates to 1888?

A. Prescott Frontier Days.

——— ?¿ ———

Q. What other Arizona rodeo claims equal longevity, but not as many continuous, admission-paid performances?